Is Austerity Gendered?

The Future of Capitalism series

Diane Perrons

––––––––––

Is Austerity Gendered?

polity

First published in 2021 by Polity Press

Polity Press
65 Bridge Street
Cambridge CB2 1UR, UK

Polity Press
101 Station Landing
Suite 300
Medford, MA 02155, USA

ISBN-13: 978-1-5095-2695-6
ISBN-13: 978-1-5095-2696-3 (pb)

A catalogue record for this book is available from the British Library.

Library of Congress Cataloging-in-Publication Data
Names: Perrons, Diane, author.
Title: Is austerity gendered? / Diane Perrons.
Description: Cambridge, UK ; Medford, MA : Polity, 2021. | Series: The future of capitalism | Includes bibliographical references. | Summary: "A devastating account of how women bear the brunt of crisis and austerity"-- Provided by publisher.
Identifiers: LCCN 2020032877 (print) | LCCN 2020032878 (ebook) | ISBN 9781509526956 (hardback) | ISBN 9781509526963 (paperback) | ISBN 9781509526994 (epub)
Subjects: LCSH: Recessions--Social aspects. | Financial crises--Social aspects. | Women--Economic conditions. | Sexual division of labor.
Classification: LCC HB3718 .P47 2021 (print) | LCC HB3718 (ebook) | DDC 306.3/6082--dc23
LC record available at https://lccn.loc.gov/2020032877
LC ebook record available at https://lccn.loc.gov/2020032878

Typeset in 11 on 15 Sabon by
Servis Filmsetting Ltd, Stockport, Cheshire
Printed and bound in Great Britain by CPI Group (UK) Ltd, Croydon

For further information on Polity, visit our website: politybooks.com

To my children and grandchildren, and in the hope of a more equitable and sustainable world.

Contents

Acknowledgements

Thanks to the three anonymous referees for their very helpful comments; to George Owers and Julia Davies for their editorial work and patience; and to the production team at Polity, especially Manuela Tecusan for her extremely diligent and timely copy-editing. I would also like to thank the UK Women's Budget Group for their permission to reproduce Figures 2.1 and 4.1, as well as for their work on austerity and the COVID-19 crisis; to the many people participating in the various webinars that took place during the lockdown, in particular those organised by IAFFE and UN Women, from which I have learned a great deal; to students on the Feminist Economics course at LSE, where many of these ideas were first presented; to my colleague Ania Plomien, with whom I have collaborated over the years; to Diane Elson, for many informative

Acknowledgements

walking talks; to Amanda Shaw for research assistance; and to Robin Dunford, for his very valuable comments on an earlier draft. All errors and misunderstandings are mine.

1

Introduction

Austerity, Gender and COVID-19

At the time of writing the world is in the midst of a global pandemic caused by a highly contagious coronavirus: corona, or COVID-19.[1] This disease has resulted in hundreds of thousands of deaths worldwide, a dramatic decline in economic activity and unprecedented increases in public deficits and debt as countries respond to the immediate health crisis and associated economic collapse.

So why ask now whether austerity is gendered? There are two key reasons. First, the cuts in health and social services during the preceding era of austerity meant that societies were ill prepared for the pandemic; and, second, when the immediate health crisis passes, there are likely to be new rounds of austerity to pay back the public debt, and they will have all the gendered and discriminatory impacts outlined in this book, unless there is a profound change in economic thinking and policy. So it is critical to show how unjust and gendered austerity is and why policymakers fail to notice or take account of these injustices. Even more importantly, as societies attempt to rebuild after this crisis, it is crucial to recognise that there are alternatives to austerity that are much more likely to resolve the problems austerity is designed to address and more likely to lead to equitable and sustainable outcomes. As Arundhati Roy has argued, the world is facing a rupture and

> a chance to rethink the doomsday machine we have built for ourselves. Nothing could be worse than a return to normality. Historically, pandemics have forced humans to break with the past and imagine their world anew. This one is no different. It is a portal, a gateway between one world and the next. We can choose to walk through it, dragging the carcasses of our prejudice and hatred, our avarice, our data banks and dead ideas, our dead rivers and smoky skies behind us. Or we can walk through lightly, with little luggage, ready to imagine another world. And ready to fight for it.[2]

In this book I consider the rationale for choosing a different world by demonstrating, in chapter 2, the gendered and unjust impact of austerity; by explaining, in chapter 3, how the economic thinking that justifies austerity is gendered; and by discussing, in chapter 4, some of the alternatives to austerity. My focus and perspective come from the global North, and especially from the United Kingdom, my own location; but austerity is a worldwide policy, often enforced by international financial institutions (IFIs) with parallel gender impacts, so I try to engage with the issue at a more global level by drawing on illustrations from elsewhere. In this introduction I outline what austerity is, the context in which it was introduced in the early twenty-first century and how the coronavirus crisis brought it to an abrupt end in 2020, but simultaneously created circumstances in which it is likely to be reintroduced.

Austerity can be defined as a conscious policy designed to reduce public deficits and debt by cutting public expenditure or raising revenue or both. 'Public deficit' refers to the annual shortfall between government expenditure and government revenue, while 'public debt' refers to the accumulation of deficits over time, or the long-term government debt. It is thought that reducing public deficits and debt through austerity programmes will secure economic stability, so that economic growth will resume. Almost always austerity is practised in ways that lead to cuts in public sector services, in public sector employment and in social protection – that is, in policies designed to reduce poverty throughout the life cycle; and all these cuts disproportionately disadvantage women, low-income people and BAME (black, Asian and minority ethnic) groups, all of whom are more likely to be reliant on the public sector for employment, services and supplements to low or no incomes.

The contemporary era of austerity began in 2010, when public deficits and debt had reached what was considered to be unsustainable levels. This happened after governments attempted to stimulate economies in the aftermath of the 2008 financial crisis, which originated in the United States and United Kingdom and left many banks and financial institutions with vast amounts of debt and unable to pay their creditors. Potential investors were unable to borrow; 'ordinary people' could not withdraw their savings and were said to be only two hours away from being unable to get cash from ATMs.[3] As these economies ground to a halt, there were fears of a total economic breakdown not only in Europe and the United States but in many other countries, as the impact of the crisis was transmitted via international financial markets and trade.

In response, the major economies around the world – the G20[4] – coordinated their activities, bailed out the banks and introduced stimulus packages to prevent economic collapse. The International Monetary Fund (IMF) supported these measures and urged governments to 'follow whatever policies it takes to avoid a repeat of a Great Depression scenario',[5] a comment almost identical to the pledge made by leaders of the G20 in 2020 'to do what it takes' to address the health crisis and economic collapse caused by COVID-19.[6]

So in 2008 the G20 agreed to spend vast sums of public money to bail out the banks and much smaller sums to restimulate their economies. Overall, 137 countries increased their public expenditure between 2008 and 2009 in order to fund the stimulus and to bail out the banks.[7] The stimulus packages varied across countries, but generally included investment in physical infrastructure and support for manufacturing to increase male employment, which had been hit first by the crisis. Social expenditure designed to protect the most vulnerable was also increased, though to a lesser extent. South Africa, Finland and the United States increased their social spending by more than 40 per cent, the average being 24 per cent for medium- and low-income countries and 27 per cent for high-income countries, between 2008 and 2009.[8] However, the size of the stimulus packages was completely overshadowed by the amount of public money lent to the banks. In the United States, the financial sector was given more than $5,000 billion, by comparison to just $829 billion received by the stimulus package – a sum equivalent to only 15 per cent of the bank's handout. In Japan, the Republic of Korea and Australia, the stimulus programme was given 25 per cent of what the banks were given,[9] while in Europe the banks received the equivalent of 36.7 per cent of European Union GDP, the stimulus programme only 1.5 per cent GDP.[10]

Bailing out the banks meant that there was a massive transfer of public funds to the private sector, that is, funds went from the public as a whole to banks, bankers and financiers, who were primarily responsible for the crisis. Ten years later this debt has been repaid fully only in the United States. Elsewhere the bailout is expected to remain a burden on the public for many years to come.[11] As Christine Lagarde, then CEO of the IMF, recognised, the bankers have enjoyed 'impunity, at a time when real wages continued to stagnate'.[12] But, while the inequality was noted by the IMF, it has not been acted on in any significant way. For low-income countries states are asked to provide a social floor to protect women and the poorest people in society; but these requests, in contrast to economic measures, are not enforced.

Then as now, in the case of the response to COVID-19, the stimulus programmes (and bailout) increased public expenditure just at the moment when state revenues were going down as a result of declining economic growth and falling tax revenues, thereby leaving governments with rising public sector deficits and escalating public debt. In 2010, the IMF pointed to the 'largest worsening of the fiscal accounts since the Second World War' and observed that austerity – or, in its more euphemistic formulation, 'fiscal consolidation' – was vital to saving economies from total collapse. As a consequence, 115 countries around the world (76 developing countries and 39 high-income ones) embarked on austerity.[13]

This rapid turnabout from stimulus to austerity, from Keynesianism to neoliberalism, led to 'austerity fever, a strange malady that combined extravagant fear with blithe optimism'.[14] The fear was that economies would fall off a cliff if public debt exceeded 90 per cent of GDP,[15] and the optimism was based on the idea that reducing government spending would generate economic growth.[16] The resulting policy has been termed 'austerity for prosperity' or 'expansionary fiscal contraction' and was based on the belief that, through a contraction of the 'fiscal space' – that is,

7

of the amount of money the government can spend – public sector deficits and debt will fall, the confidence of creditors will increase, interest rates will fall, and the public sector will stop crowding out the private sector, which will resume investing, thereby regenerating economic growth. This belief – that contraction would lead to expansion – is clearly oxymoronic in a literal sense, and did not work in practice. Evidence shows that countries practising austerity barely grew, and in some contraction led to an overall decline. Greece, for instance, recorded a decline of 25 per cent in GDP per capita between 2007 and 2013. Even in 2017, GDP remained 23 per cent lower than its pre-crisis level.

Nonetheless, governments around the world were fairly successful in persuading people that austerity was essential and that it would be in everyone's long-term interest. One tactic was to pursue an analogy with household budgets. For example, the UK government argued that the country had 'maxed out its credit card' and that we (the country) would now have to 'tighten our belts'.[17] By so doing, it diverted attention from the mismanagement of bankers and financiers insofar as it implied that the debt was due to the profligacy of the state. This strategy made public spending and the corresponding debt appear to be the cause rather than the consequence of the crisis and provided a rationale for cuts in public spending – and thus for austerity.[18] The argument has a commonsense appeal: if you are in debt, you have to cut back in order to pay back. But this analogy between state finances and household budgets is completely false in economic terms. As Keynesians as well as heterodox and feminist economists argue, economies are different from households. In an economy, one person's spending is another person's income and vice versa; so, if everyone tries to save and pay off debt at the same time, there is no money for spending and hence no demand for products, which leads to a deepening of the recession.[19] So, in times of recession and low growth, governments should spend public money to restimulate economies, as indeed they did in the immediate aftermath of the crisis and as they are doing at present, in response to the economic decline associated with COVID-19. The rationale for this alternative perspective is discussed in chapter 3.

Austerity policies were implemented in over two thirds of the world in the aftermath of the 2008 financial crisis, but austerity is not restricted to this period. Typically, governments respond to crises with short-term stimulus packages; but then, as soon as the immediate problems are resolved, they implement austerity policies to claw back the debt. In the 1980s and 1990s the IMF enforced a policy of structural adjustment – austerity – on many indebted medium- and low-income countries, especially in Latin America and sub-Saharan Africa; in the late 1990s similar policies were recommended to countries in South East Asia after the Asian financial crisis. Towards the end of the second decade of the twenty-first-century austerity was practised in Argentina, Chile and Ecuador, as well as in eleven states in sub-Saharan Africa, in response to growing public debt and as a condition for securing IMF loans. Even in Guinea and Sierra Leone, both of which were only just recovering from the Ebola crisis of 2013–16, the IMF programmes required reductions in the health budget and in other services such as care, gender-based violence prevention and social protection; it also imposed cuts on food and fuel subsidies.[20] In 2015, the Brazilian government froze real public expenditure at 2016 levels for the next twenty years. This policy was endorsed by the IMF but described in the *Washington Post* as 'the mother of all austerity plans' and by the UN as 'an attack on poor people'.[21] Despite the intensity of this policy and the severe implications for the well-being of the population, the policy has had no success to date. GDP is 5 per cent lower than it was in 2016 and unemployment has risen from 4.8 per cent to 12.3 per cent. The principal aim of the policy – to reduce public deficit and debt – also failed, as both have risen owing to the continuing decline in economic activity and to falling tax revenues.[22] In 2018, twelve countries in sub-Saharan Africa – including Ghana, Zambia and Zimbabwe, as well as Afghanistan and Moldova in Asia – were at high risk of debt distress, and all were compelled by the international financial institutions to introduce austerity.[23] So, while varying considerably across countries in terms of timing and extent, austerity has become an almost automatic response to public debt, despite its failure.[24]

Austerity had in effect become the 'new normal',[25] until it came to a sudden and unforeseen end in 2020, when the coronavirus pandemic hit. It began in the province of Wuhan in China in late 2019 before spreading, in early 2020, to other Chinese provinces and countries in East and South Asia, for instance Singapore, Republic of Korea, Taiwan, Japan and India. The epicentre of the pandemic then moved, by turns, to Italy, Spain, the United Kingdom and other European countries, then to the United States and, next, to countries in South America and Africa. Government responses to the corona crisis have varied, but all governments

11

spent huge amounts of public money to address the immediate health emergency and its adverse socioeconomic consequences and to forestall economic decline. Overall, 193 countries implemented some form of stimulus package;[26] and the scale of these packages and of the corresponding amounts of public expenditure, borrowing and accumulated debt far exceeded those that followed the financial crisis.[27]

There was widespread recognition among governments and IFIs that this level of stimulus and debt was necessary in order to counter the immediate health crisis and to forestall further economic decline,[28] but it is unclear what will follow. Many activists and scholars see the crisis as an opportunity to 'build back better' and establish a more sustainable and gender-equitable model of development.[29] Some governments and international institutions have mentioned using the stimulus to fund a green new deal to mitigate climate change. Nonetheless, there is a real risk that, after brief attempts to stimulate economies, there will be a return to 'normal' – and this would mean new rounds of austerity, with all the unjust and gendered impacts about to be outlined in this book.

Already in the conditions attached to IMF loans granted to low-income countries for the purpose of combating COVID-19 there is an expectation that, once the immediate crisis is over, there would be a swift return to 'fiscal consolidation'.[30] Likewise, the UK Treasury drafted a paper that proposed public sector wage freezes designed to claw back the deficit, despite the fact that the workers in these sectors risked their lives by acting in key public-facing roles during the pandemic, especially in health and social care. They were and continue to be disproportionately women and BAME people, and they are, in a literal sense, vital to society.[31] The corona crisis has unveiled how these front-line public sector workers play a crucial role in maintaining the essential fabric of social life, a role now widely recognised; and this recognition took public form via coordinated evening applause across the globe, from China, where the crisis started, to Italy, Spain, France, United Kingdom, Switzerland, Turkey, Peru and Brazil.[32] Hopefully the momentum of these emotional tributes will be built upon and will translate into decent terms and conditions for the workers, long-term funding for these sectors and a more gender-equitable future, but this remains to be seen.

Austerity appears to be an abstract, gender-neutral economic policy, but in practice it is gendered in two distinct ways. First, women and men play different roles in the economy and in the home, and so they are affected differently by economic and social policies. Second, austerity policies reflect a particular kind of masculinised free market thinking that prioritises the health of 'the economy' over and above social welfare and, perhaps not unwittingly, serves the interests of high-income elites. So austerity is gendered not only because the outcomes of policies are unequal and tend to disadvantage women disproportionately, but also because the economic thinking that underpins austerity is profoundly gendered.[33] Gender is differentiated by social class, age, race, ethnicity, citizenship status, (dis)ability, sexuality and other markers of social distinction and disadvantage that, together with geographical location and state policies, make the experience of austerity very different depending on who you are, where you are and what you do.[34] What becomes clear, however, is that, while the way in which austerity is gendered is variable and contingent, the fact that austerity is gendered is not.[35]

2

The Gendered Impact of Austerity

If you got a group of misogynists in a room and said guys how can we make this system work for men and not for women they would not have come up with too many other ideas than what is already in place.

Philip Alston, UN rapporteur[1]

Austerity is gendered because it creates a triple jeopardy for women.[2] Women lose more jobs, more services and more social protection than men owing to the stereotypical and indeed real differences in the economic and social roles that women and men play in the economy and in the home, the social norms that sustain these gender differences, and the failure of macroeconomic policies to recognise the significance of such norms. In this chapter I discuss the three issues listed just now: loss of jobs, loss of services and loss of social protection. I then highlight how cuts are cumulative, increase the amount of unpaid work that women do and contravene international human rights conventions because they cause undue harm while not being absolutely essential.[3] First though, I discuss the uneven gender division of labour within paid work and between it and caring. This division varies among countries but is nonetheless universal and represents one of the main and most enduring sources of gender inequality and injustice. It is a key reason why austerity is gendered.

The uneven gender division of labour between work and care

Paid work

In the labour market, women face segregation and discrimination as well as limited access. Even in 2018, there are eighteen countries where husbands can prevent their wives from doing paid work, and overall 2.7 billion women are prevented by law from doing the same jobs as men.[4] Paid work is universally segregated: vertically, by status and, horizontally, by sector, occupation and contract. Women and men work at different levels in the jobs hierarchy and do different kinds of work, which have different terms and conditions. Men are more likely to hold senior positions, women are more likely to be found lower down the hierarchy, with lower pay, in more flexible and insecure jobs, and in the informal sector. Horizontally, women continue to be concentrated in 'the 5 Cs' – cleaning, caring, catering, cashiering and clerking – while men are overrepresented in construction, manufacturing and occupations dealing with money, machines and management. While gender equality policies have been in place for many years, the pace of change is glacial. In Europe, for example, women represent 78 per cent of healthcare and social service workers, while men constitute 80 per cent of the construction workforce.[5] In rural agricultural communities and among small-scale businesses women are twice as likely as men to be family workers rather than independent employees or owners.

The extent of these divisions and their implications vary across countries, but the broad patterns are similar. This positioning, and the fact that women's overall labour market participation rate is 25 per cent lower than men's, mean that on average women are more likely than men to have lower lifetime earnings, lower or no pensions, and fewer assets and less independent access to social protection.[6] As a consequence, women, especially

low-income BAME (black, Asian and minority ethnicity) and migrant ones, have fewer resources than
men to fall back on in times of adversity.

One way in which women have tried to improve
their employment situation is by moving into the
public sector, where employment conditions are
generally better – more regular, more secure and
more gender-friendly, that is, with better equality
and diversity policies, better maternity, paternity
and parental leave, and a smaller gender pay gap.
But austerity has blocked this route through massive
cuts in public sector employment and pay. Another
potential escape is by becoming self-employed
(although self-employment can be disguised employment, that is, a means by which employers transfer
the risks and costs of employment to employees)
or by running micro-, small and medium-sized
enterprises.[7] Microenterprises have expanded in
lower- and medium-income countries, particularly
in Bangladesh and India, and are seen by the World
Bank and others as a means of raising women's
income and empowerment, though evidence suggests
that the empowering impact has been very mixed.[8]

Many enterprises and jobs in the service industry,
where women are disproportionately concentrated,
have been adversely affected by lockdowns associated with COVID-19 and this has caused them

extreme hardships, as their livelihoods were suddenly gone; and the same happened to people in the informal sector.[9] In India, for example, the unexpected lockdowns, together with the suspension of public transport, forced many migrants – men, women, and their children – to walk for hundreds of miles in order to get back to their villages, as these were now their only hope of securing survival, even though they had worked for many years in the cities.[10]

Deep-seated gendered social norms also mean that, when jobs are scarce, women are more likely than men to lose theirs. In the Asian financial crisis of the 1990s, women in the Republic of Korea were seven times more likely than men to lose their jobs.[11] In several EU countries such as Greece, Spain, Ireland, the United Kingdom and Portugal, women's employment fell below the 2005 levels after the 2010 austerity programmes. Although their employment has increased subsequently, the new jobs are more likely to be in the private sector and to have more precarious terms and conditions.

Emerging evidence indicates that women's employment has been hit more adversely than men's by the lockdowns associated with COVID-19. This is due to the overrepresentation of women in the hospitality, retail, arts and cultural sectors, which were severely hit and slow to recover. This gender imbalance exists even though women are massively overrepresented (+70 per cent world-wide) among the front-line workers who fight the virus, for example nurses or workers in residential care, and among support workers such as cleaners and laundry workers, all of whom are at greater risk from exposure to the virus.[12]

In the United Kingdom, in the first two months of the crisis, there was a disproportionate number of deaths among BAME people working in the NHS. They accounted for 64 per cent out of 119 deaths, although this group represented only 20 per cent of the workforce. The reasons for this imbalance are still being investigated, but BAME people are disproportionately present in front-line positions as well as having a disproportionate tendency to suffer from underlying health conditions; and both these factors are linked to underlying structural socioeconomic inequalities.[13]

Care and domestic work

On average women spend over 2.5 as much time as men on domestic and caring work; and the uneven distribution of these responsibilities furthers their disadvantages in the labour market.[14] This difference varies across countries. Among OECD countries, the smallest differences between women and men are found in the Nordic countries, while those in Italy, Japan, the Republic of Korea and Portugal are much larger; and even in the Nordic countries the differences are far greater in this area than in childcare.[15] This gender gap limits the types of jobs that women can do and the amount of time for which they can do them. Yet both domestic and care work are 'vital to individual socialization and the reproduction and maintenance of people upon which the economy depends'[16] and, if valued, these kinds of work would contribute between 10 per cent and 39 per cent of GDP.[17]

This essential economic and social contribution is not recognised by orthodox economists. Hence, when cuts are made in public expenditure, they often fall on these services and disadvantage women disproportionately, through loss of jobs and the increase in unpaid care work that arises as a consequence. Women are far more likely than men to be the ones who fill in the gaps in service provision; and they may reduce their paid work or withdraw from the labour market altogether in order to do so. This is a product both of social norms, which consider caring roles to be 'women's roles', and of the gender pay gap, which means that in a heterosexual two-parent household the male is likely to be the higher earner.

Is Austerity Gendered?

The lockdowns associated with COVID led to closures – of schools, nurseries and workplaces as well as of services that supported domestic work like cleaning and general help. In consequence, the amount of childcare and domestic work that had to be done at home increased; but so too did the number of people at home, who were in theory available to do this work. This potentially creates conditions for changes in the domestic division of labour and childcare. Unfortunately the evidence from the United Kingdom suggests that the differential gender roles already in place were consolidated rather than transformed, as women picked up the increased amount of caring and domestic work associated with the lockdowns. Specifically, among two-parent households, mothers were 1.5 times more likely than fathers to have been furloughed[18] or to have lost or quit their jobs and, if they worked from home, they were more likely to be interrupted by household responsibilities. If a mother stopped doing paid work but her male partner continued, then she was found to do twice as much unpaid housework and childcare work as her male partner; but, if the reverse was the case, then housework and childcare were shared equally between the two partners, while mothers also did five hours of paid work per day.[19] Given that women's jobs have been hit disproportionately by COVID-19, there is a risk that this traditional gender division of labour between paid work and caring might be reinforced.[20]

Some care work can never be commoditised and some can be pleasurable, but this does not explain why it cannot be shared more evenly between women, men and the wider community or why it cannot be valued economically. It constitutes a time tax on women and results in their having less access to money and finance, and therefore fewer resources with which to withstand austerity. It also lowers women's independence, their voice in household and community decision-making, their presence in positions of power and influence – including in economic policymaking – and reflects and reinforces unequal power relations between women and men.

The lack of representation in decision-making not only deprives women of opportunities but also deprives society of more balanced and potentially better decision-making. In the case of the coronavirus pandemic, women have been particularly evident in leading roles in countries such as Germany, New Zealand, Denmark, Finland and Bangladesh, which have managed the crisis well by locking down early and by containing the virus more effectively, which resulted in fewer deaths than elsewhere. These specific illustrations are supported by statistical evidence from 194 countries that shows significant and systematic differences between countries led by women and countries led by men.[21] Angela Merkel, the German chancellor, is on record with this comment: 'caution is the order of the day, not over-confidence'.[22] This view contrasts markedly with the approach taken by the leaders of United Kingdom, United States and Brazil – who, at least at an early stage, dismissed the seriousness of the virus and prioritised preserving the economy over protecting health. In consequence these countries have experienced very high rates of infection and death.[23]

While it is true that social norms tend to encourage values such as confidence, strength and daring in men and caution and caring among women, this is not to suggest that women and men have fundamentally distinct natures; indeed academic research shows that women and men have similar dispositions regarding risk[24] – and in fact other countries with male leaders, for example Greece and the Republic of Korea, have managed the current crisis quite well. Rather the argument here is that greater diversity in all spheres matters, because differently situated people have different experiences of life, are affected differently by socioeconomic policies, are likely to see the world in different ways, and taking account of these varied positions is likely to lead to a better informed and more representative decision-making. I now return in greater detail to the specific jeopardies associated with austerity, many of which undermined the capacity of countries to deal with the corona crisis and people's resilience to its effects.

First jeopardy: Cuts in public sector jobs, pay and conditions

Cutting public sector employment and the wage bill is one of the quickest and easiest ways of reducing public expenditure. In 2010, 130 governments planned to follow this path. Among them were the United States, nineteen European states and ninety-six medium- and low-income countries from other parts of the world. In 2015 Brazil and Argentina jumped on the bandwagon.[25]

These cuts are gendered, because women's share of public sector employment generally exceeds their share of total employment. In OECD countries, women accounted for 58 per cent of the public sector workforce, but only of 45.3 per cent of the overall workforce.[26] In the United Kingdom, the public sector workforce, two thirds of which consist of women, has been cut by 11 per cent between 2010 and 2018; but local authority employment has been cut by 30 per cent,[27] and this includes social care and teachers, where women and BAME are overrepresented to an even greater extent. By contrast, central government employment, which has a higher proportion of high-level jobs in which men are overrepresented, has remained relatively stable. Similarly, in the United States front-line workers, especially Afro-Caribbean women, were more likely to lose their jobs than white and Hispanic workers, even when controlling for factors such as levels of education, length of service and occupation.[28]

Between 2009 and 2014, in Greece teaching was cut by 9 per cent, public administration by 12.6 per cent and healthcare by 6.8 per cent. In Portugal there was a decrease of 13 per cent in public administration and one of 20 per cent in teaching. Public sector pay was also cut, either directly, through pay freezes, or indirectly, through other changes to payment systems that caused serious falls in the workers' purchasing power. In Greece, public sector workers experienced a 40 per cent loss in purchasing power; in the United Kingdom teachers experienced a loss of 9 per cent.[29] Elsewhere in lower-income countries reductions in funding from international and local donors led to similar retractions in the social sector throughout this period. In South Africa, for example, community-based organizations providing health and social services were particularly affected, which led to job losses and lower incomes for women.[30]

These cuts demoralise existing employees. Their jobs and pay become insecure; they face an increasing volume of work with fewer resources and they witness increasing deprivation among their clients, as those, too, experience the negative impacts of austerity.[31] To meet the continuing demand, many public sector workers do unpaid overtime and use their own money to mitigate shortfalls. In the United Kingdom a survey carried out for the Teachers Union NASUWT found that nearly 50 per cent of teachers had bought classroom materials as well as food and other necessities for their pupils, even though they were 'facing financial hardship themselves as a result of year-on-year pay cuts'.[32] Other workers leave these sectors for more rewarding conditions elsewhere. In 2020, the United Kingdom registered a shortfall of 100,000 workers, including nearly 40,000 nurses in the NHS, and a further shortage of 122,000 workers in the social care sector.[33] These shortages were exposed by the pandemic. They led to the cancellation of operations and services not connected to COVID-19 and prompted pleas from the government for recent retirees and leavers to return to the sector.[34]

Second jeopardy: Cuts in public services

As public sector jobs are cut, the quality of services almost inevitably falls. This decline is intensified by direct cuts in public spending on services and by outsourcings to the private, for-profit sector. Privatisation is thought to increase efficiency, but the imagined gains often prove elusive, because many public services are highly labour-intensive, which means that it is difficult to reduce costs without reducing quality simultaneously. Years ago an economist asked: How would you increase the productivity of a string quartet, as it will always take the same amount of time to play?[35] The music could be speeded up, but almost certainly would not be as good. Care work has similar economic properties.

Contemporary technologies allow for some productivity gains. For example, concerts can be recorded and transmitted virtually; but, for the recipient, this is not the same as being there. Likewise, as the corona crisis has shown, some teaching can be delivered online and doctors can carry out consultations via video. New technologies, including robots, can also be implemented for simple tasks. For example, in the area of elderly care, they can be used to monitor temperatures, to issue reminders for taking medicines, and even to keep people company, as has been done in Japan. But virtual contacts cannot completely replace the benefits of human interaction.[36]

More generally, many public services are inherently labour-intensive because they are relational, never routine, and always likely to require thoughtful and unpredictable responses, so there are limits to the number of people whom any carer, teacher or health worker can assist simultaneously. This is why it is simply not possible to increase the productivity of individual workers in this area as it would be, for example, in manufacturing. In consequence, wages form a higher proportion of the total costs, and the relative cost of public services rises over time with increases in the cost of living or in the minimum wage, even though these workers are among the lowest paid. These characteristics also mean that, while public services are essential to overall well-being, most people would not be able to afford their full market price – which is why in many countries they are subsidised, funded or provided directly by the state.[37]

Rather than recognising the economic properties

of caring services, neoliberal politicians often think that the rising costs are due to public sector inefficiencies and can be resolved through privatisation. But private suppliers face rising costs too, just like the public sector. Hence they find it difficult to make a profit, unless they charge high prices and restrict provision to the elite or reduce the pay and conditions of the workers, especially if public funding is cut or fails to match the rising costs. In addition, the profit motive mitigates against investment in and preparation for uncertainties, including pandemics.

In the United Kingdom, local authorities are largely responsible for funding the largely privatised social care sector; but central government has cut the funding of local authorities by nearly one third since 2010, when austerity began, and by up to one half when inflation is taken into account.[38] Some private sector providers have demanded more funding in order to be able to maintain service quality and working conditions.[39] Other companies continue to make a profit, but they do so primarily by reducing the quality of care provided and by lowering the pay and the standards of working conditions. When a private equity firm, Care UK, took over a contract from the National Health Service to run community care services for people with learning disabilities, it imposed pay cuts of up to 35 per cent and reduced the pay for new employees to the minimum wage. Given that women are overrepresented among care workers, they were disproportionately affected by these cuts. Some employees left and others went on strike. The husband of one of the women on strike commented:

> She is up at night worrying about paying the bills ... People are going to have to leave. They are bringing in people on £7 an hour who often don't want to do this sort of job. You have to pay the bankers their bonuses to keep the talent. Is this not as important or more important – keeping these people safe?[40]

The government also proposed to cut childcare costs by increasing from four to six the number of toddlers (i.e. children aged between 12 and 36 months) whom each carer is allowed to look after. To highlight the absurdity of this suggestion, Zoe Williams, a journalist, published a picture of herself trying to look after six toddlers simultaneously.[41] In the end the government did not pursue this idea. It has expanded instead the number of free nursery hours per child in order to encourage mothers to move into paid work, but it did so without adequate funding, making it difficult for nurseries (which are largely private) to maintain quality.

Apart from cuts in the work force and in the pay, service quality can be reduced by measures such as discharging people from hospital early,[42] shortening school hours, and raising the eligibility criteria and threshold for intervention. Yet another way to diminish care quality is by worsening the conditions for the remaining workers – by making them work harder, faster and more flexibly, for instance. As a care worker commented, 'you try not to hurry them or to let them know you haven't enough time but you are aware that your next client is watching the clock and waiting for you to arrive'.[43]

Costs can be sometimes reduced by closing down public services altogether. Without any kind of impact assessment, the UK government has made severe cuts to the Sure Start programme, which had provided a one-stop service in health, education and childcare for toddlers under five years. Subsequent research has shown that the activity of Sure Start centres led to a significant reduction in the hospitalisation of children later on, especially in disadvantaged neighbourhoods, which meant in turn lower costs for the National Health Service. This case illustrates the male-biased, short-term and gendered thinking prevalent among policymakers, who fail to recognise the economic as well as the social value of care work.[44]

Cuts to the support for survivors and victims of violence against women and girls

One of the most gendered and least visible cuts is support for survivors and victims of violence against women and girls (VAWG), which is a serious and pervasive human rights violation. Domestic violence affects all societies, social classes and cultures and impacts on women unduly. More than one third of all women in the world experience some form of physical or sexual violence (or both) throughout their lifetime mainly from their male partners or former partners, and almost half of all female victims of murder are murdered by an intimate partner. The comparable figure for men is 1 in 20 (i.e. 5 per cent).[45] These figures understate the true extent of violence, as many victims and survivors remain silent owing to male impunity, to women's economic dependency on their partners, and to the discriminatory and patriarchal attitudes in society that consider male violence to their female partners a normal part of everyday life.[46]

The coronavirus pandemic has increased the risk of VAWG through lockdowns: these are associated with economic distress and home isolation, conditions that heighten the likelihood of violence while simultaneously increasing the powers and impunity of perpetrators by making escape and access to legal services and places of refuge more difficult. Emerging evidence indicates that 80 per cent of the 49 countries surveyed by UN Women reported increases in VAWG. These include Malaysia, up by 40 per cent, China and Somalia, up by 50 per cent, a 79 per cent increase in Columbia, and a 400 per cent increase in Tunisia.[47] In addition, cases of VAWG have risen between 25 and 35 per cent in France, Cyprus, Singapore and Argentina.[48] The increased demand for help, coupled with concerns about the spread of the virus and social (and physical) distancing, has left the services that address the VAWG problem overstretched; and these conditions were made worse by underfunding during the preceding era of austerity.

The 2015 Brazilian austerity programme resulted in a 58 per cent reduction in spending on services that specifically benefitted women and a 15 per cent cut in the support for survivors of sexual or domestic violence.[49] No new shelters are being established, in a country where the rate of femicide is the fifth highest in the world and where the impact of the pandemic has been among the worst on the globe. In the United Kingdom femicide doubled in the first three weeks of the lockdown and calls to helplines increased by 50 per cent.[50] While the government has provided some new funding, it by no means compensates for the cuts made during the period of austerity. Overall, between 2010 and 2020 there was a 17 per cent decrease in specialist refuges; 60 per cent of the women who sought support were unable to be housed; and one in four domestic abuse refuges lost all government money for therapeutic support.[51]

Although governments have taken some steps to respond to the increased demand for shelters, what is now needed is long-term fully funded strategies designed to prevent VAWG and to secure sufficient refuges and other services for survivors. These services need to be run by people with experience and knowledge of violence against women; they also need to be led by the needs of service users and recognise that these needs may differ among different groups of women. At present these services are in a critical condition in many countries despite the increase in need, despite resistance and protests from women, and despite research that demonstrates the high costs of domestic violence on the economy as a whole.

The full cost of domestic violence in the United Kingdom has been estimated at £66 billion a year by government researchers. This figure covers protective and preventative measures, physical and emotional harms, the lost output, and the costs incurred by health and victim support services as well as by the police and the criminal justice system. If only a small percentage of this sum were spent on preventing domestic violence and providing support for those who seek to escape and survive, the change would be dramatic.[52] Not only do austerity policies create real social harm, but in many cases they do not even save the money they are supposed to save.

Third jeopardy: Loss of social protection

The impact of reductions in public sector employment and services is intensified by losses in social protection, that is, by cuts to safety nets that support people who otherwise have little or no means of securing their livelihoods. In 2010, 68 medium- and low-income countries and 39 high-income countries planned to cut social protection by eliminating, reducing or freezing existing measures. Many European countries, including Greece, Spain and Ireland, raised the pension age. Later in 2015, Brazil froze all social spending for 20 years in real terms; it also reduced women's services by 58 per cent[53] and cut or severely reduced two flagship social protection programmes that targeted cash payments to women. Bolsa Verde, 88 per cent of which was paid to women in rural regions in return for protecting the environment, was cut altogether, while Bolsa Familia, a more broad-based programme directed at the poorest households with children, was downsized by 10 per cent between 2014 and 2017, women being 93 per cent of the recipients.[54]

From 2010 on, successive coalition and conservative governments in the United Kingdom made unprecedented cuts to social protection. Existing systems of support were terminated and caps were introduced to ensure that households could not receive more from social protection than from working, regardless of their circumstances. The majority of the affected households – 94 per cent – had children, and 72 per cent were lone parents, overwhelmingly women. The government also brought forward planned measures to equalise the retirement age between women and men and, simultaneously, extended the pension age. While moving towards greater gender equality, these changes were to the severe disadvantage of women, who had to work much longer than they had anticipated.

In addition, a new online system was introduced: Universal Credit. This system was designed to simplify existing arrangements but also made the criteria for obtaining funds more stringent. People with disabilities were assessed regularly for their 'work-readiness' by private firms that were incentivised to get people off benefits and whose employees had little or no medical training. Subsequently, 8 per cent of their reports were found to be inaccurate and in conflict with medical evidence and led to appeals, 60 per cent of which were successful. This raised doubts about whether this approach actually cut public expenditure,[55] although overall people with disabilities who were relying on social protection lost 30 per cent of their net income between 2010 and 2018.[56]

Sanctions, including the loss of funds for periods of three months or more, were applied to all those who infringed the regulations, which people living precarious lives often found difficult to meet. Officials had some flexibility in the case of lone parents, in recognition of their caring role. But these relaxing measures were not written into the regulations; they were therefore at the discretion of individual officials and depended on their goodwill. In 2016, 22 per cent of lone parents were sanctioned and, even though 62 per cent of appeals were successful, the whole process took time, compounding parental stress and making children suffer throughout lengthy periods, often as a consequence of government mistakes; besides, not everyone appealed.[57] These rules were relaxed during the COVID crisis, as the difficulty of meeting the conditions was recognised, but were re-imposed in June 2020, even though meeting the conditions remained extremely difficult, especially for people with disabilities.

The system was also highly gendered, in that payment was made only to the main earner. This discriminates against a second earner, who in a heterosexual family is likely to be the woman; hence by the same stroke it undermines women's financial independence. In principle payments could be split between partners in cases of domestic violence, but this provision highlights the designers' lack of gendered knowledge, as it would be difficult, if not impossible, for people to press such a claim safely when they are experiencing domestic abuse – which includes financial coercion.

Overall, the social protection budget was cut by nearly 25 per cent, even though the cost of living increased; and one should bear in mind that 80 per cent of the 'savings' secured through these cuts came from women.[58] In an intersectional analysis of the changes in taxes and benefits since 2010, the Women's Budget Group, together with the Runnymede Trust, showed that the cuts fell disproportionately on women, especially on lone parents and BAME women, and caused a dramatic fall in their standard of living. More specifically, when compared to low-income white men, low-income BAME women lost twice as much money. They lost much more by comparison to high-income white men, mothers and single mothers losing the most (see Figure 2.1).[59] Among the poorest households, losses were particularly heavy for Asian women, who saw almost 20 per cent of their income vanish. Black women lost 14 per cent and white women 11 per cent of what they would have earned if austerity had not replaced policies existing at the time. Overall, the poorest 30 per cent of households lost 12 per cent of their disposable income, while the richest 30 per cent suffered no loss at all.[60] This pattern of distribution made it clear that the strongest negative impact of cuts in social protection hit those least able to bear it: low-income people, low-income women, and especially low-income BAME women, who constantly experience other forms of structural discrimination as well – namely in employment, education, health, housing and care.[61]

These cuts in social protection triggered growing

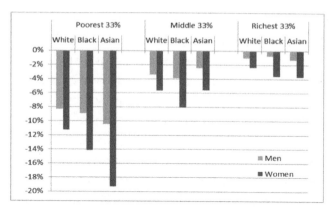

Figure 2.1. Impact of changes in taxes and benefits, 2010–20, United Kingdom

Source: WBG and Runnymede Trust with Reclaim and Coventry Women's Voices (2017)
Note: The figures reflect the cumulative individual impact of changes in taxes and benefits as a percentage of net individual income per annum by household income groups, gender and ethnicity.

risks of food and fuel poverty, homelessness and indebtedness and prompted a 52 per cent increase in the use of food banks in areas where Universal Credit had been introduced; in other areas the use of food banks increased too, but only by 13 per cent.[62] A large proportion of users were lone mothers, a fact that gives us another indication as to the gendered character of austerity.

The UK government justified austerity by attributing public debt not to the 2008 bank bailout but to the profligacy of the welfare state. It claimed that public money earned by hardworking people, the 'strivers', was being handed out to 'skivers', people who were living extravagant lives at the strivers' expense and undermined competitiveness and economic growth.[63] This representation may have contributed to the development of an 'anti-welfare common sense' that stigmatised recipients and legitimised deep cuts in social provision.[64] Such ideas of individual rather than social failure can be internalised, and when this happens they undermine any sense of entitlement and promote self-doubt, isolation, poor mental health, and even acts of suicide – all of which increased after 2010 and are statistically associated with austerity.[65] With the pandemic, many more people are now dependent on some form of government support and optimistically this may undermine the negative portrayal of people relying on social protection.

Austerity and human rights

Austerity increases joblessness and deprives people of the services and social protection that might otherwise have mitigated these effects; its general result is a lowering of standards of living – especially for women, minority groups and those who are already poor. Legally states are not committed to guaranteeing any particular standard of living; but austerity policies are incompatible with human rights obligations, if they mean that people are 'deprived of essential foodstuffs, [of] primary health care, of basic shelter and housing, or of the most basic forms of education'.[66] Such policies signal that states are failing to discharge their obligations under the International Convention on Economic Social and Cultural Rights (CESCR), which was signed and ratified by the majority of states, though not by the United States, as well as under the Convention on the Rights of the Child (CRC) and the Convention on the Elimination of all forms of Discrimination against Women (CEDAW), which were signed up to by 187 states. These conventions recognise that resources are not unlimited, but they commit states to working progressively towards creating an environment that enables human flourishing and to using all available resources to this end. If resources are limited, then priority should be given to those people who are the most deprived. If states fail to meet these obligations when they have the necessary resources, they are guilty of *retrogression*: in other words they move backwards, in terms of rights and resources, from an existing situation – and they do so when alternatives exist.[67]

Conventions are not legally binding unless implemented through national legislation; but states have to report on the extent to which human rights are being secured or violated, and UN rapporteurs monitor state performances. Their reports serve in naming and shaming states that violate human rights or fail to move progressively towards targets; and campaigners use these reports to press for progressive change.[68] Rights conventions can also be used as yardsticks to evaluate proposed policy changes and policy outcomes, but this is done inadequately – on the rare occasions when it is done at all.[69] The UN rapporteur described the United Kingdom's austerity programme as chaotic, cruel and vindictive – a programme that resulted in poverty for a significant part of the population. When introducing the report at a press conference, he also argued that the programme was misogynist.[70]

The UK government rejected the findings of this report,[71] even though between 2010 and 2018 it had cut social protection by £37 billion while simultaneously lowering taxes by £57 billion and thereby violated the conventions, since not all resources were drawn upon to ensure that existing rights were maintained.[72] The combination of these policies was a highly gendered product: it effectively transferred 'money from the purses of poorer women into the wallets of richer men'.[73] While these measures are differentiated by social class and BAME status, on average women are more likely to suffer from cuts in social protection than men – whereas men, whose incomes are on average higher, are more likely to gain from lower taxes. Far from everyone 'being in it together', as the government claimed, this was rather a case of creating a stimulus for the more affluent and serving austerity to the poor.

Coronavirus crisis and the end of austerity?

Cuts in public sector employment, services and social protection are dangerous and damaging. They are highly gendered, economically illogical and driven by a very narrow neoliberal economic agenda, which prioritises economic growth and stability above all else. The weaknesses of this agenda were exposed in early 2020 by COVID-19, the most serious global pandemic for generations. The lack of fully functioning health and care systems, together with high-density, inadequate and overcrowded housing, poor water supplies, inequality and poverty, meant that, although everyone was and, at the time of writing, still is at risk, the impact of the virus was differentiated by gender, age, social class, BAME and migrant status.

Data worldwide suggest that, all in all, there have been more deaths among men than among women and among older people than among the young. In the United States, BAME people have been much more seriously affected than non-BAME people. Likewise, in the United Kingdom one third of the critically ill patients were in the BAME category, which accounts for only 14 per cent of the population, and the death rate among them was twice as high as among the white population.[74] Generally speaking, the impact of the virus varied by type of work and by housing situation. People with white-collar jobs and on higher-pay scales were more likely to be able to work from home and to have access to more space in and around their homes, so they came into physical contact with fewer people. By contrast, those lower down in the pay hierarchy – and women were predominant among them – were more likely to be employed as key workers in health, social care, transport and food production, to depend on public transport, to live in more crowded accommodation, and hence to be much more exposed to the virus. The lockdowns reduced the transmission of the virus for people who were able to apply the rule of social distancing.

But, for those living in densely populated cities, in the favelas of Brazil or in the slums around Indian cities, the lockdowns represented lost income and, once the virus was present, they left people dangerously exposed to it.[75]

In response, governments across the globe abandoned austerity and embarked on programmes of unparalleled public spending, in an attempt to mitigate the worst effects of COVID-19. These programmes varied across countries but, in addition to spending on health care, they consisted largely of measures designed to prevent people from becoming destitute, make it possible for businesses to stay afloat, and generally support the economy and save it from total collapse.[76] This about-turn also demonstrates that austerity is a political choice and not a technical necessity, an argument developed further in the next chapter.

COVID-19 has been, first and foremost, a health crisis, but also one that floored economies all around the world. Out of the 189 members of the IMF, 170 expected to have negative growth at least during the second and third quarters of 2020, if not beyond, and 193 countries implemented stimulus programmes.[77] While it is usual for stimulus programmes to follow economic crises, as we saw happening after the financial crisis of 2008, the magnitude of the public sums spent to mitigate the worst effects of the virus was unprecedented. After the immediate crisis has passed, however, it is also usual for countries to try to recoup this expenditure and pay off the accumulated debts by imposing some form of austerity. Thus, only two years after the 2008 financial crisis, concerns about the rising levels of public spending led to an abrupt turna-round, in which austerity, with its very uneven and gendered impacts, became the 'new normal' – until 2020.[78] If this is not to happen again, it is critical that the gendered economic thinking that justifies austerity is now displaced by alternatives.

3

The Austerity Deception

Gendering Economics

> The purpose of studying economics is not to acquire a set of ready-made answers to economic questions, but to learn how to avoid being deceived by economists.
>
> Joan Robinson (1955: 75)

Austerity is one of the most monstrous deceptions of our time. It devastates millions of lives across the globe and has particularly acute consequences for low-income people, women, BAME people, and people with disabilities or any kind of social disadvantage. At the same time, austerity policies generally fail to reduce public debt or restore economic growth, and thus fail to fulfil the purpose for which they were introduced. So why are such policies so prevalent and persistent in spite of their damaging and gendered character, let alone their lack of impact on economic recovery? And why is

49

there a risk that, after the immediate effects of the coronavirus crisis disappear, austerity will return, even though there are more inclusive, gender-equitable and effective ways of repaying public debt and restoring economic growth? Why does the austerity deception persist?

To address these questions, it is necessary to study at least some aspects of economics. In this chapter I consider how some economists and policymakers justify austerity by drawing on neoliberal economic theory and how this theory and the related macro-economic policies are gendered. I illustrate how feminist economics recognises the gender biases inherent in this perspective and shows that auster-ity is a political choice, not a technical economic necessity; moreover, it is a choice that prioritises the interests of the affluent and powerful elites over the well-being and rights of everyone else.

Neoliberal and feminist understandings of the economy

Neoliberal economists see the economy as an amoral and complex machine with millions of interacting parts; these parts are coordinated by Adam Smith's 'invisible hand', and the result is said to be optimal outcomes for all.[1] Any state interference with this market mechanism is thought to be doomed to fail, because nobody would be able to orchestrate these parts effectively.[2] To expect that would be the equivalent of asking a small child to dismantle a clock and rebuild it.[3]

The key to market efficiency is *Homo oeconomicus* – the (supposedly rational) economic human, who makes decisions on a logical basis, in his or her own interest. As Adam Smith, the founder of free market economics, argued,

> It is not from the benevolence of the butcher, the brewer, or the baker, that we expect our dinner, but from their regard to their own interest. We address ourselves, not to their humanity but to their self-love, and never talk to them of our necessities but of their advantages.[4]

This perspective stresses the virtues of leaving the free market economy alone. State intervention, funded by taxes, is believed to undermine individual freedom and to prevent markets from working effectively. If people pay too much in taxes, they will have less money to spend on private sector goods and less money to save. If savings are too low, there will be no money for investment and growth will not take place. Hence high taxes and high public expenditure are believed to crowd out the private sector and to distort free market outcomes, on which individual freedom and economic dynamism are thought to depend.

Neoliberal theory has a very narrow, androcentric conception of the economy. It focuses on the production and consumption of goods and services in the market. In the view of its proponents, production and investment take place primarily through market-oriented firms and entrepreneurs, and the role of the state should be limited. Households are assumed to provide labour for the market and to consume market goods with the incomes they receive, or else to save. No account is taken of the fact that households produce some goods and services and that it is in them that labour is reproduced.

Given the imagined virtues of free markets, neoliberal thinkers believe that in times of recession it is better to wait for the market to right itself, even though this may take a long time. So, if people are unemployed, it is best to let wages fall until it is profitable to employ them again. That is, the self-regulating market will right itself in the long run. It is somehow forgotten that people are not commodities like soap or shoes, but real living beings, who will die unless wages are high enough to fund sufficient food, shelter and clothing.

By contrast, John Maynard Keynes pointed out that state action is necessary in order to prevent the waste and hardship caused by idle resources – including unemployed people; he pointed out that the market could take a long time to right itself, and 'in the long run we are all dead'.[5] Keynesians and feminist economists argue that, far from its being the case that public or state spending takes money out of people's pockets, thus crowding out the private sector, in reality it puts money into people's pockets and in this way encourages spending, puts idle resources to use, stimulates the private sector and ensures that the economy reboots itself and life continues.

Feminist economists also recognise the materiality of everyday life and argue that the protagonist of neoliberal theory – this rational economic human who makes decisions entirely on the basis of self-interest – is a fiction. They ask where this rational economic human came from, how he was raised, and 'who cooked his dinner'.[6] More specifically, feminist economists critique this atomistic, independent, self-interested portrayal of human behaviour and the idea that, if left to itself, the market will produce socially optimal outcomes. They also reject a narrow, market-based understanding of the economy. They point out instead that, in reality, human beings do not come to the economy fully formed; they do not just emerge 'from the earth like mushrooms' and grow up 'without any obligation to each other'.[7] Rather, human beings are nurtured and cared for by others – typically by women, who provide most of the caring labour at work and in the home, all throughout life. Feminist economists claim that people live interdependently, that every person needs someone to care for him or her at some stage in life. Societies need production and social reproduction, so these are interdependent elements of the economy.

Social reproduction includes all the activities involved in caring, some of which may be hidden from view, but nonetheless play a vital role in ensuring the existence of healthy, educated and well-nurtured citizens and workers.[8] Economies simply would not function without this reproductive work. Through caring and nurturing, people develop the values and capabilities necessary for engaging in society and in the economy as affective and effective citizens and workers. Thus social reproduction in the home makes an important and productive contribution to the economy, no less than in the paid sectors of care, health and education, or manufacturing. For this reason, such work should be recognised as a productive economic activity. If the resources for it are not replenished, they will be depleted[9] – which is precisely what happened during the era of austerity. The chronic underfunding and understaffing of public services weakened the capacity of states to deal with the COVID-19 pandemic.

At the macro level, neoliberal theory sees the economy as a separate entity independent of society, almost an inanimate being defined by abstract macroeconomic variables such as debt, deficit, inflation, interest and growth rates – all of which need to be kept within certain bounds to ensure economic stability regardless of their social and gendered impact. Neoliberal economists assume that, if these variables are managed correctly, economic growth will be high and will trickle down and benefit everyone. While the notion of trickling down has been critiqued extensively, given the very high levels of inequality within and between countries, the idea of ensuring that these macroeconomic variables should remain within certain boundaries is central to neoliberal theory and justifies austerity.[10]

In the neoliberal model of development, gender differences are not paid any attention and social policies are sidelined in times of economic crisis. There is an implicit assumption that the economy creates wealth; but caring activities, insofar as they are considered at all, are regarded as costly and consuming rather than creating wealth; hence the belief that they must be cut in order to reduce debt and restore growth. The possibility that social policies are economically productive, or that economic policies favour some groups more than others, is overlooked in conventional economic thought.[11] Unless the assumptions underlying these economic ideas are exposed, it will be extremely difficult to realise gender justice in any substantive ways.[12]

Feminist economists see the economy in a more rounded way, as consisting of production and reproduction and as having the purpose to secure well-being by providing what societies need. They argue that it is important for society to select priorities and exercise influence over resource allocation accordingly instead of relying on the market to produce socially optimal outcomes. In their view the economy should work for society rather than the other way round. In effect neoliberal and feminist economists have very different understandings of what the economy is and what it is for. While neoliberals focus on ensuring that the economy works to produce profit by making things and increasing GDP, feminist economists focus directly on life-making activities that support societies from one generation to the next.[13]

In the feminist perspective, tax is not something

that will drain resources away from, or crowd out, the market but a contribution that people make to ensure that everyone can have access to necessary services such as health, education and care, on which overall well-being depends. The rich cannot protect themselves completely from crime, fires and infectious diseases such as COVID-19, so they, too, depend on high-quality social infrastructure. Employers need physical and social infrastructure: transport and telecommunications on one side, healthy and educated workers on the other. Indeed, these are some of the reasons why public inter-ventions have evolved over time, leading to state investment and to the creation of the contemporary welfare state, at least in high-income countries.[14] A US Democratic Party politician remarked:

> There is nobody in this country who got rich on their own. Nobody. You built a factory out there – good for you. But I want to be clear. You moved your goods to market on roads the rest of us paid for. You hired workers the rest of us paid to educate. You were safe in your factory because of police forces and fire forces that the rest of us paid for. You didn't have to worry that marauding bands would come and seize everything at your factory... Now look. You built a factory and it turned into something terrific or a great idea – God bless! Keep

a hunk of it. But part of the underlying social contract is you take a hunk of that and pay forward for
the next kid who comes along.[15]

In reality, only the staunchest free market sup-
porters advocate a totally free economy and a very
narrow role for the state. Moreover, their idealised
self-regulating market has rarely if ever existed,
because in practice it is unsustainable.[16] Economics
textbooks recognise, along with Adam Smith, that
there are many areas where the market does not
work and where state action is necessary to ensure
optimum outcomes; such general areas are, for
example, education, health, care, environmental
protection and public infrastructure – and more
specific areas in the latter are roads, telecommunications and street lighting. Indeed, one of the
enduring characteristics that distinguish individual
states is given by the precise balance between the
state and the market; thus the state plays a major
role in China, in the Republic of Korea and other
parts of South East Asia, in the Nordic countries,
and to some degree in Germany and France, while
in the United States and United Kingdom the role of
the market has greater prominence.

Even so, in the last four decades until 2020 –
with the exception of the period 2008–10, when
states embarked on stimulus packages – the role of

markets has been increasingly emphasised, while that of states has been confined mainly to ensuring the necessary conditions for markets to function, namely safeguarding the realm, guaranteeing contracts and stabilizing, privatizing and liberalizing the economy. And it is this latter aspect – ensuring economic stability – that has dominated contemporary economic policy and lies at the heart of austerity programmes. But to ensure that markets function can mean massive state intervention, as demonstrated by the huge amounts of money lent or given to the banks in 2008 – and, again, in 2020, when even greater amounts of public money were spent on protecting health and preventing economic collapse. So the real question is, what kind of intervention should there be? Would it be one designed to assist the markets, the large corporations and the banks, or one aimed at supporting strategies that directly prioritise and promote the health and well-being of everyone, in more gender-equitable ways?

The neoliberal case for austerity: Fiscal space, public debt and gender biases

To expose the austerity deception, I now outline the neoliberal case for austerity before explaining its inherent gender biases. Within the neoclassical perspective, economic stability depends on the size and sustainability of 'fiscal space' – the amount of money a government has available to spend. Fiscal space is portrayed graphically in Figure 3.1 by the diamond area. Three of the corners show possible sources of finance. These consist of external grants or debt relief, which are applicable mainly to low-income countries; domestic revenue mobilisation, namely tax or proceeds from privatising public assets; and deficit financing, that is, borrowing from capital markets, creditors and international financial institutions (IFIs) such as the International Monetary Fund (IMF), the World Bank or the European Central Bank. The fourth corner represents government spending.

Fiscal space is elastic: each corner of the diamond can be pulled in different directions, the shape at any moment depending on the level of spending and on the specific sources of finance. Reflecting a neoliberal perspective, the IMF defines fiscal space as the 'room in a government's budget that allows it to provide resources for a desired purpose without jeopardizing the sustainability of its financial position or the state of the economy'.[17] High public deficits and debt are thought to jeopardize a government's financial position and to threaten economic

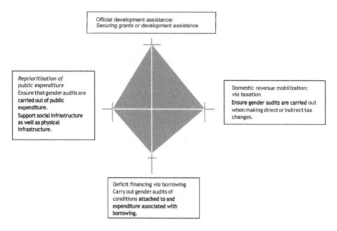

Figure 3.1. Gendering fiscal space

Source: Modified from UNDP 2007; see also Perrons 2014: 217.
Note: There are few technical constraints on the size and shape of the fiscal space; rather the space could be pulled in different directions, depending on political priorities. Neoliberals prioritise 'economic stability' and favour a minimal role for the state, with low government expenditure, low taxation and low debt. Feminists argue for a proactive state, with state investment for securing social goals that are subject to gender audits in order to ensure gender equity in the use of public funds.

stability. More specifically, they are thought to undermine creditors' confidence, owing to fears that the government could default and fail to repay the debt. As a consequence, credit agencies lower the credit rating of countries with high public debts, which leads to higher interest rates and increases the costs of future borrowing. Or it may become impossible to borrow from anyone except the IFIs that impose specific conditions. In reality there is little evidence to support the view that creditors will not buy up public debt, especially in higher-income countries, where they can be relatively confident that the debt will eventually be repaid. Nonetheless, it was these concerns about debt that led to fiscal consolidation (austerity); and they are the reason why the IMF expects states to follow austerity in the future, as a way of lowering the accumulated debt caused by COVID-19 once the immediate crisis is over.[18]

Overall, in 2010 the IMF and the Organisation for Economic Co-operation and Development (OECD) urged countries towards fiscal consolidation in order to stop the spiralling of debt. This prompted 115 countries (39 high-income and 76 developing countries) to instigate austerity policies, either as a result of the conditions attached to IMF or other IFIs loans or in the belief that they would reduce debt and restore economic growth. In general, states attempt to reduce debt by raising revenue, by cutting public expenditure, or through some combination of the two. But there are many different such combinations, and they have different distributional implications. Most governments have cut public spending and raised taxes in gender-biased ways, perhaps not with a conscious intention of doing so but as a consequence of following an abstract economic model that fails to recognise the materiality and gendered structure of everyday life.

Raising revenue

If governments decide to raise revenue, they can increase taxes, privatise public assets and services or adopt a combination of both methods. Given their belief in the greater efficacy of the private sector, neoliberals prefer privatisation. Some German MPs suggested that Greece should sell the Acropolis and the islands, but the more usual approach is to sell public utilities and services. Portugal sold leases on airports as well as postal services. Greece sold long-term leases on its main ports and airports and was encouraged to privatise water supplies, together with Ireland, Italy and Spain. Several countries such as Greece, Ireland, Latvia, Portugal, the United Kingdom and Spain have been privatising parts of the health service, in an attempt to reduce public spending and create freer markets in the health sector. They did it sometimes by introducing user charges, even though, when set against the administrative costs, such charges yield few returns and have adverse impacts on care.[19] The privatisation of health services also discriminates against women, who are less likely to be able to pay and yet more likely to be in need, especially for reproductive health services. In addition the profit motive mitigates against investment in preventative care for the mass population. Overall, 55 countries engaged in some form of privatisation between 2010 and 2015 – 15 high-income countries and 40 lower income ones. These practices are continuing, as they form part of the conditions attached to subsequent IMF loans;[20] for example, the 2015 Brazilian government planned to privatise the postal services and to sell parts of the public stake in the oil industry in order to raise revenue.[21]

Privatising public utilities raises money in the short term, but potentially valuable public assets are transferred from the public – in principle, from everyone – to private buyers, which means that the future income stream from these assets will go to private shareholders rather than back to the state, where it could fund further investment in public services. Privatisation also leads to higher user charges, and hence discriminates against those on low incomes, because paying for basic utilities such as fuel and water becomes a greater share of their income.

In lower-income countries, the privatisation of water not only puts prices up but also limits pipe extension, making women and girls, who traditionally fetch water, walk greater distances. This increases the amount of unpaid work they do and puts their health and safety at risk. Privatisation also causes variations in the quality of provision and leaves the poorer people with the underfunded public services left over, or sometimes with no services at all – because it is less profitable to supply services to the edges of cities, to shanty towns or to people on low incomes, where the risk of non-payment is higher.[22]

The problems arising from the lack of clean running water in the overcrowded outskirts of cities – in favelas, slums and refugee camps – were cruelly exposed during the COVID crisis, when people living in these areas were unable to take even the most basic preventative advice of regular hand washing. Given the relevance of contiguousness to this coronavirus, the lack of water provision increases the risk for everyone. Interestingly, it was the intention of limiting the spread of infectious diseases that first led to the state's involvement in water provision in nineteenth-century United Kingdom.

Privatisation is also associated with job losses, wage cuts and compromises in service quality; and there is little or no evidence of any increase in efficiency resulting from it. These problems have prompted public service suppliers in several areas – for example, the water utilities in Berlin and Paris – to take back control from private suppliers, although around the same time the German state was demanding that Athens and Thessaloniki privatise their own supplies (to date, public protests in Greece have prevented full water privatisation).[23] Even the extremely pro-neoliberal UK conservative government has decided to renationalise aspects of its probation service, owing to irredeemable flaws found in private sector provision and to the steep increase in costs that they caused.[24]

Besides privatisation, many countries tried to resolve the debt problem by raising taxes, but there are different ways of doing it and they have different distributional effects. Governments could reduce tax evasion and avoidance or could make large and highly profitable companies pay more tax. They could raise tax rates for top earners or levy a Tobin tax on financial transactions.[25] Even a minuscule levy would raise significant sums, given the volume of financial transactions. This tax would also be some recompense for the consequences of the financial crisis – which are attributed in part to unregulated financial transactions. Instead of these progressive policies, governments invariably choose to increase consumption taxes such as value added tax (VAT), because these can be implemented quickly and are difficult to evade. Thus 138 countries increased their consumption taxes between 2010 and 2015. But consumption taxes are highly regressive, hence they have a greater negative impact on low-income people – and especially on women, who form a greater share of the low-income population.[26]

In 2010 the United Kingdom raised VAT to 20 per cent (from 17.5 per cent in 2008); but, as pointed out in chapter 2, other taxes – including corporation tax, fuel duties and income tax – were reduced. This produced an overall tax reduction of £57 billion a year, which was greater than the amount of money cut from the social protection budget, namely £37 billion a year.[27] The combination of tax and benefit cuts in the United Kingdom meant that these measures had little overall effect on reducing the debt but a significant distributional effect on the poor, on women, on BAME people and on people with disabilities, all of whom they disadvantaged. Indeed, this effect suggests that the financial crisis was used as an excuse for the government to pursue its deep-seated conservative agenda of reducing state support and making people more dependent on the market, despite the regressive distributional implications of such an agenda.

Cuts in spending

As taxes are thought to undermine personal free-dom, neoliberals focus on cuts to public expenditure to reduce debt. Once again, there are different ways in which this can be done. Governments could reduce defence spending and cut the salaries of high-earning government officials on the one hand, or reduce subsidies, social protection, pensions, public sector pay and services on the other. It is these latter policies that have been the most prevalent. From 2010 on, 132 countries planned to limit subsides, often on fuel and food; 130 countries cut or capped the public sector wage bill; and 107 countries put in place measures to reduce social protection and pensions, often by adjusting the eligibility criteria, for example by raising the age at which pensions become payable.[28]

Besides doing real harm to those who can least afford it, all these measures have a 'deflationary' bias because they remove money from the economy and thereby lower its growth.[29] No priority is given to maintaining full employment or providing high-quality public services. Moreover, despite being presented under the guise of penalising no group in particular and eventually benefitting all, this bias is gendered, because it is public spending that provides the jobs, services and social protection on which women disproportionality depend, given the enduring and unfair gender division of labour between paid and unpaid work, as discussed in chapter 2.[30] These measures are also biased against people on low incomes, who are more likely to depend on subsidies and social protection. Again, such people are mostly women, especially BAME ones and people with disabilities.

As neoliberal policies prioritise economic stability over well-being, they 'prevent the formulation of gender-equitable people-centred macroeconomic policies'.[31] In effect they present what is a political and gender-biased choice as a technical economic necessity. The majority of policymakers simply do not see, or choose not to see, the gender implications of their policies. As noted in chapter 2, the UN rapporteur for poverty in the United Kingdom thought that misogynists could not have designed any better policies to disadvantage women. But, when he asked those responsible for the reforms in social protection whether there was a gender dimension, 'they (the ministers and officials) looked at each other and say no, no I think the policies are fair'.[32] This response indicates a surprising lack of knowledge about, or wilful neglect of, information that is already in the public domain.

In 2010 the Fawcett Society brought a case

against the UK government for failing to meet its legal duty to examine the equalities impact of the budget. It provided evidence showing that 72 per cent of the government cuts had fallen on women. The judge conceded that the government had not carried out the necessary impact assessment; yet he failed the case because it was 'academic' and conflicted with the needs of the government and global business.[33] Subsequent research showed that over 80 per cent of the cuts had fallen on women, and a House of Lords Select Committee highlighted how the Treasury had failed to meet its legal duty to carry out the necessary equalities analysis of the budget, arguing that its own analysis should be evaluated by independent experts to show how it could improve its performance.[34] The Treasury should perhaps consult the UK's Women's Budget Group (WBG), whose members have been analysing the gendered impact of government budgets for many years.[35]

Gender-responsive budgeting

Gender budgeting started as a radical demand made by feminist groups, but is now advocated by international institutions such as the OECD and the IMF, and over 80 countries engage in some form of gender budgeting, though often in a cursory way. At its best, gender-responsive budgeting 'demystifies the apparent gender neutrality' of the budget and exposes the gender biases in macro-economic decision-making.[36] More specifically, it aims to identify the gender-differentiated impact of government revenue-raising and spending policies. It can also help to design more gender-equitable and sustainable alternatives by making well-being, women and human rights the target of analysis rather than economic stability. At a governmental level, Canada has probably made the most progress. Its 2018 budget examined the differential impact of its policies on gender equality and on the minority population, monitored the outcomes of policies, and formulated plans to redress the inequalities it identified.[37]

The WBG, together with the Runneymede Trust, estimated the intersectional impact of austerity by gender, race and class and showed clear regressive biases, as low-income BAME women were experiencing the harshest impacts of austerity (see chapter 2 Figure 2.1). The WBG has also analysed the gendered impact of the COVID-19 crisis and, to date, its analysis has been far more sophisticated than anything done by the UK government, despite the fact that the latter has a legal public duty to conduct equalities impact assessments and despite the huge difference in the resources available to the two parties – the WBG being a small group run primarily on a basis of voluntary labour with occasional donor contributions.[38] The biases identified by the WBG belie the governmental claim that 'we are all in this together' – a claim revealed to be false during austerity and, again, during the COVID-19 crisis. Nonetheless, the UK government continues to disregard this research. But, even so, such analyses do provide the foundations for designing more equitable and sustainable policies.

The United Kingdom's lack of attention to gender issues is surprising, as most countries, including those affected by austerity, have gender equality policies. Many have subscribed to the Committee on the Elimination of Discrimination against Women (CEDAW) and other conventions for gender equality and committed to gender mainstreaming, which requires that all policies be examined for their gender impact, both before and after they are introduced. The European Union, which promised to practise gender mainstreaming in 1996 and aimed to apply it to 85 per cent of all new initiatives by 2020,[39] seems to forget gender when economic issues are considered. For example, the European Union's Economic Recovery Plan, drawn up in the wake of the financial crisis, failed to mention gender even once.[40] This neglect highlights the priority given to the economy and shows that, in orthodox neoliberal thought, this concept – the economy – is understood in a narrow, androcentric way.

Feminist economists' understanding of fiscal space and alternatives to austerity

Feminist economists take a different approach to the economy and to public expenditure. Returning to Figure 3.1, fiscal space can be described as the available financing, designated, through policy choices, to provide the necessary resources for a set of social, economic and environmental objectives; and it should take into account the specific needs of marginalized groups using race, gender and class impact analysis.[41] So, in principle, there are always different ways of managing the elements portrayed in Figure 3.1; these ways are economically feasible, but 'different strategies imply different distributions of the costs and benefits'[42] and hence have different gender implications. This alternative definition makes reference to social purpose and to the idea of using public funds to support those in greatest need. As a result, the political nature of economic decision-making is made explicit, as is the idea that the economy should work for people rather than vice versa.

This feminist perspective therefore takes the view that, in complete contrast to the stability rules of the European Union and to IMF policies, there is no fixed size for fiscal space. While governments rarely run up deficits and debt indefinitely, not least because large amounts of public money would have to be spent on interest repayments to creditors, there is no known limit as to what a maximum amount might be.

Austerity is a deception; it is portrayed as an economic necessity, when it reality it is a political choice that disadvantages low-income people and women in particular. The underlying rationale of austerity depends on neoliberal economic ideas that are gender-biased. These ideas favour free markets over state involvement and overlook the way in which economic life and social life rely on human interdependencies and on reproductive work that requires collective or state involvement.

The neoliberal view that governments should always balance their budgets – in other words that they should have no debt and, preferably, should run a surplus – does not capture the only possible option. Heterodox and feminist economists describe this perspective as anti-deficit radicalism[43] and point out how it defies the basic logic of economics.[44] Borrowing, provided that it is well used, can generate returns in the future and can contribute to economic growth and well-being. Given that the present levels of public borrowing are high, it is critical that this public money be used in ways that support people throughout the COVID-19 crisis, but also contribute to developing alternative strategies for resolving the problems and inequities of the current economic system and for building back a better future.

4

Alternative Futures

Societies are in turmoil and economies are in a nosedive . . . With solidarity we can defeat the virus and build a better world.

Antonio Guterres, Secretary General of the United Nations[1]

In the midst of the coronavirus crisis there was widespread reflection on who and what really mattered and on how the existing system had resulted in deep structural inequalities between the rich and poor, between the majority population and BAME people, and between men and women and failed to meet economic or social needs. Alongside these injustices, the ruinous impact of economic activity on the environment was spectacularly revealed: the lockdowns led to a significant drop in carbon emissions, cleaner air, clearer waters and quieter cities.

The virus had exposed the consequences of

austerity, and especially the underfunding and understaffing of key public services such as health and social care and there was acute recognition that the key workers, those involved in life-making and life-preserving activities – nurses, doctors, care assistants, cleaners and laundry workers in health and social care, then supermarket workers, delivery and public transport drivers – were the people who really mattered and on whom society depended. Yet these workers were predominantly low paid and on precarious contracts; most of them were women, often from a BAME background, and migrants of uncertain citizenship status. During austerity these workers had been told that the cuts were essential, that there was no 'magic money tree' to finance investment in their services or to fund higher pay for the workers such as themselves. But the virus made it clear that, if the state so desired, it could expand public debt and increase public expenditure to unprecedented levels, without collapsing the economy.[2] Indeed, it was recognised that such expenditure was vital to keeping the economy going and to preserving life. There was also reflection on what might be done next, once the health emergency was over, together with much optimism that returning to 'normal' is no longer a viable option.[3] It was considered critical to 'build back better' – in short, it was time for a new deal, a new world order.

In this respect there has been a profound change in state economic policy, from austerity and neoliberalism to Keynesian-inspired stimulus programmes. But the question is, how long will this stimulus last, and what will follow it? Will this upheaval lead to a turning point, a new epoch? It certainly provides an opportunity to develop differently, but will this happen? Or will it be that, after a couple of years, we will see a return to 'normal' and to fiscal consolidation and austerity, as concerns about the scale of public debt grow? The IMF is already envisaging fiscal consolidation for the lower-income countries to which it is financing loans at the present.[4] What happens will depend very much on how the borrowed money is spent as well as on the duration of the stimulus. How long for will it last?

Many writers predict that change follows crises. Karl Polanyi, writing in 1944, argued that, 'undoubtedly, our age will be credited with having seen the end of the self-regulating market',[5] and after the 2008 financial crisis Eric Hobsbawm commented similarly: 'It's the end of this particular era. No question about it. There will be more talk about Keynes and less talk about Friedman and Hayek

... We now know that the era has ended. [But] we don't know what's going to come.'[6]

While Polanyi's prediction was realised between 1945 and 1975, the neoliberal self-regulating market economy, which justified austerity, re-emerged and dominated economic policymaking for the next four decades, until the 2020 coronavirus crisis, with a brief respite over the period of stimulus between 2008 and 2010 – thus invalidating Hobsbawm's prediction.

There are many proposals for alternative futures circulating at present, and it seems that more people are open to radical suggestions for change, although the risk of a return to austerity remains. The question is how this desire for change can be translated into practical policies that will preclude a return to 'normal'. Arguably, change is more likely when there is demand for it before the crisis, when this demand for change grows during the crisis, and when the responses to the crisis contain elements that prefigure the future strategy.[7]

In this chapter I consider forms of resistance to austerity and demands for alternatives that predated the COVID-19 crisis or, in some cases, were developed as it unfolded. These forms and demands range from adjustments to the neoliberal austerity agenda through Keynesian-inspired alternatives within capitalism to more transformative agendas. Arguably all the strategies I consider here are potentially more inclusive than the current practices, but not all recognise the gendered dimensions of austerity and economic policymaking; yet these dimensions must be addressed if fully inclusive and gender-equitable strategies are to be designed and implemented.

Austerity, resistance and demand for change

Academics, think tanks, charitable organisations and NGOs wrote many texts that analyse and demonstrate the negative impacts of austerity, and some of these texts deal with its gendered impacts.[8] Even the IMF has expressed some reservations about how austerity was practiced, given its negative effects on gender equality and on low-income populations – and especially the unanticipated consequences of the cuts in public expenditure on economic growth among these populations.[9] As a consequence, the IMF has encouraged states to maintain safety nets and to reduce debt by raising tax revenues, alongside cutting some of their expenditure. But these more egalitarian measures are given far less priority than debt cutting; and, as the IMF continues to press for fiscal consolidation once the health crisis is over, there has been no fundamental change in thinking. There have been, though, many protests against particular aspects of the cuts.

In Iceland, where the scale of the banking collapse after the financial crisis of 2008 was the greatest any country has ever experienced relative to its population size, a 'pots and pans revolution', sustained over five months, pushed the president to call for a referendum. It also determined the election of a new, more gender-balanced left green coalition government. As a result, the bankers were sent to jail rather than being bailed out with public money. While the new government met the IMF's conditionality criteria to reduce public debt, it did so in a more gender-sensitive manner and more in line with human rights. Rather than making deep cuts in social protection, it tried to preserve the well-being of the most marginalised while increasing the tax contribution of the top 40 per cent. Even so, child benefit was cut temporarily and employment policies were addressed more to men than to women, partly because men, who are over-represented in construction industries, were the first to lose their jobs, but also as a consequence of social norms that prioritised the significance of these jobs, given men's assumed role as primary breadwinners.[10] The government also committed to gender-responsive budgeting in order to analyse the impact of its policies on gender; but, to date, this kind of budgeting has been practiced only in Reykjavik, the capital city. To the surprise of neoliberals, Iceland was the first country to recover from the financial crisis.

In 2018, the Argentinian right-of-centre government announced a new round of austerity that resulted in massive cuts to public spending and reduced subsidies for food and fuel and large layoffs of public sector workers. These cuts led to the closure of services such as community health centres, which had provided free prenatal and infant care as well as support for many thousands of women and transgender survivors of domestic violence.[11] While the government acknowledged that poverty would increase, it nonetheless claimed that it would continue to protect children, though it is difficult to see how this can be done with reduced services. The scale of austerity led to massive protests and, in 2019, to the election of a leftist government.

When the coronavirus hit, this new government introduced an early lockdown, and COVID-19 cases were lower than in Brazil. The government decided to use all available public funding to address the health crisis and, in so doing, had to default on existing debt repayments. As Joseph Stiglitz commented, 'Argentinians want to pay what they owe to the extent they are able to pay, but you can't ask people to die in order to pay creditors.'[12] This government also supported Ni una menos (Not One [*sc.* Woman] Less), a movement originating in Argentina but active in many countries of Latin America in their struggle against austerity and the rising costs of living and in support of women's rights. The primary focus of this movement is to end violence against women and girls (VAWG); but, in Argentina as elsewhere, the lockdowns led to large increases in reported cases of VAWG.[13]

In the United Kingdom there was intense opposition to austerity from movements such as Occupy and UK Uncut as well as from the main opposition party, though not until 2015. Several women's groups of various orientations campaigned against cuts, discrimination, sexual harassment and VAWG; and they did so locally, nationally and in conjunction with international campaigns. Here are three prominent participants: Sisters Uncut, whose members protested against the rising number of deaths from VAWG by shouting 'Dead women can't vote' beside an art installation of the women's suffrage movement, near the parliament; Southall Black Sisters, an organisation that has been challenging racism and sexism for more than forty years; and Focus E15, a campaign group that fought consistently for social housing ever since 2013, when twenty-nine single mothers evicted from their own homes in east London occupied some vacant buildings and displayed a banner that read 'These homes need people, these people need homes.'[14] The struggle of Focus E15 ended successfully, as an affordable housing charity took over the proposed redevelopment from the private for-profit sector. But, despite such occasional successes, austerity continued until 2020.

In parallel with the Occupy movement in the United States and in the United Kingdom, the Indignados in Spain and many feminist groups all over the world protested about violence against women and about the numerous cuts – in social protection, in care provision for children, the elderly and the infirm, in jobs, in pay, and in improvements to working conditions. In 2017 Las Kelly's, a group of hotel cleaners, campaigned against falling wages, increasing workloads and the habit of outsourcing to agencies and promoted hotels with good labour practices on TripAdvisor. In France, women marched against austerity in 2013, in the aftermath of cuts in public healthcare, pay freezes in the public sector, and an increase in VAT. From 2018 on many women have participated in the *gilet jaune* (yellow vest) movement, protesting against austerity and the high costs of living. All these measures affect women more drastically than men, because the social protection system is based primarily on a model of the male breadwinner, which puts women at a disadvantage in the labour market and leaves them underprovided. In 2013 the Greek ministry of finance sacked nearly 600 directly employed women cleaners in Athens and outsourced their jobs in order to meet the European troika's demands for cuts in public spending. The women camped outside the ministry in a sustained struggle, using red rubber gloves to symbolise their jobs and their resistance. These jobs were reinstated in 2015 by Syriza, the incoming leftist government; but, reflecting other examples, this victory against particular cuts did not produce a change from the broader package of austerity,[15] and in 2019 the centre-right parties regained power in Greece. Many of these movements coordinate and march on the International Women's Day, in protest against the failure of states to ensure the realisation of rights to which they have already committed.

These are just some of the protests against austerity and in favour of a fairer and more equalitarian society. They are very uplifting for participants, occasionally successful, and critical to maintaining the momentum of opposition. But, even though such movements seem very powerful at the time and sure to bear results, unless they lead to a change in government they tend to be transient and fragmented and are often forgotten. Thus, although there have been many protests against austerity and the existing system of economic and social regulation, resistance has been largely unsuccessful to date. Arguably Extinction Rebellion, a nonviolent international environmental movement with mass support, especially from young people, and Black Lives Matter, which came to renewed prominence during the pandemic, after the death of George Floyd at the hands of a US police officer, have influenced current thinking about building a better, greener and fairer future, both among some politicians and in the wider public; but it remains to be seen how much these proposals will translate into policies and will include gender equality.

Towards alternatives to austerity and alternative futures

Adjustments to the existing system
One aspect of the current system that needs immediate change is the mode of financing debt, especially for lower-income countries. Given the current

pandemic, the G20, the International Monetary Fund (IMF) and the World Bank have called for the prioritisation of health expenditure and social protection, have advanced new loans, and have suspended their own debt service charges; but these measures follow austerity programmes that caused disinvestment in, and the underfunding of, health and other public services.

In 2020 governments around the world accumulated deficits and debt to levels that would have been considered unthinkable in 2010 and went far beyond the 90 per cent of GDP that had been claimed to lead to total economic meltdown, thereby justifying austerity. In the United Kingdom public debt was already equal to 100 per cent of GDP in June 2020; in the United States it was 107 per cent, in Brazil 100 per cent, and in Italy 155 per cent. Likewise, public deficits exceeded the recommended levels.[16]

In lower-income countries the role of the state is generally less extensive and, while public debt has increased significantly, the overall levels are lower. But loans to these countries are considered to be riskier, so interest rates and the costs of servicing debt are much higher. The loan conditions often require that some of the loan be used to pay back creditors. In Ghana, the IMF and the World

Bank provided $1.7 billion in loans for the period 2015–19; but the same amount was spent on debt servicing to private lenders, with levels of interest between 8 and 10 per cent, while public expenditure was cut by 17 per cent.[17]

The IMF estimated that the COVID-19-related loans to low-income countries could increase service costs to 30 per cent of GDP, which is clearly unsustainable; and, while the IMF has postponed debt-servicing charges until 2021, the payments will still have to be made in the future – to the IMF and to other lenders.[18] Thus the Ecuadorian government paid the service charges on its sovereign bonds (debts to creditors) in the midst of the pandemic, despite civil society protests, arguing that it had to do so as a condition for receiving new loans from international financial institutions (IFIs).[19] What is more, countries are concerned that suspending their interest payments would lower the rating they receive from credit agencies, and hence would increase the costs of raising loans with other lenders.

So, while countries are borrowing, they are also paying back large sums to creditors at high interest rates. This means that the interests of external creditors are prioritised over those of the population, even though high interest rates are supposed to reflect risk – namely the possibility that the loan will not be repaid. These conditions are highly gendered in that public service cuts impact especially low-income women, while creditors are people with much higher incomes and predominantly male.

Thus, instead of a suspension of service charges, there needs to be a wholesale cancellation of debt: this should enable countries to deal with the pandemic, repair their services broken by years of austerity, and finance new projects so as to allow sustainable and equitable growth and to escape from the continual rounds of debt and austerity. Such a move would contribute towards rebalancing the world economy.

The Bretton Woods Project has consistently monitored and critiqued the IMF's and the World Bank's actions towards lower-income countries.[20] More specifically, it recommends changes to the terms on which all loans are made and repaid – changes such as greater transparency, being subject to public accountability, and being evaluated via gender budgeting; in the absence of such transparency, states should not be required to repay the loans. Nor should they be required to pay back reckless lenders, or use new IMF loans to repay existing debt. Further, the Project recommends that any other outstanding loans should be restructured, so that countries may have time to pay them back while they enable all their available resources to be used in ways that are consistent with realising women's and human rights.[21] Overall, the Project argues for an alternative, gender-just macroeconomics and stresses the importance of the public sector provision of physical and social infrastructure. This view is shared by a number of organisations and analysts in the context of specific proposals for building more sustainable and inclusive economies and societies, proposals that have been given renewed significance through the support for progressive change after COVID-19.

Towards more transformative change

I begin by outlining the Global New Deal (GND) proposed by the United Nations Conference on Trade and Development in 2017 because it combines many suggestions put forward by various organisations to reverse austerity; and, despite predating COVID-19, it contains the seeds of a post-COVID-19 recovery.[22] Potentially it provides a framework within which we can situate proposals of feminist and other groups – proposals related to these groups' specific locations.

UNCTAD: Towards a GND

The GND aims to overcome austerity and secure the sustainable development goals (SDGs) that 193 states agreed to achieve by 2030.[23] These goals include ending poverty in all its forms everywhere, achieving gender equality and empowering all women and girls, reducing inequality within and among countries, and promoting inclusive and sustainable economic growth, employment and decent work for all – as well as ending hunger, securing clean water and protecting and sustaining the environment.

The GND seeks to correct the imbalances that created inequitable and exclusionary outcomes and to provide a strategy for transforming the SDGs from aspirations into 'decisive policy action'.[24] It requires action on a scale equivalent to, or even greater than, the Roosevelt New Deal, which lifted the US economy out of the Great Depression of the 1930s, and the Marshall Plan, which helped to resurrect European economies after the 1939–45 war, although it seeks to involve ordinary people in the decision-making process. Such a scale might have seemed unlikely when the report was written, but it corresponds to the COVID-19 stimulus programmes in many countries.

The GND is based on three interconnected

pillars: recovery, regulation and redistribution. Like the alternatives proposed by feminist and left-wing economists, it challenges the 'short term, predatory and, at times, destructive behaviour of deregulated markets', as 'prosperity for all cannot be delivered by austerity-minded politicians, rent seeking corporations and speculative bankers'.[25] Again like feminist and left-wing economists, the GND is based on a broadly Keynesian understanding of how the economy works. From this perspective, it recommends increasing state expenditure on quality public services and on social protection and increasing public investment in physical and social infrastructure,[26] research and development, health and education. Its advocates point out that a proactive state is key to recovery, as it has a much greater impact on aggregate demand and employment creation than either tax cuts or quantitative easing: these methods have been tried and, although they cost the public large amounts of money, they failed to boost any kind of economic recovery, let alone an inclusive one.

The GND also proposes greater control over financial markets and labour relations, so as to reverse the power asymmetries between private capital and the state and between capital and labour. Specifically, it seeks to establish greater control over finance and the banks in order to encourage long-term investment in the real economy and to prevent the siphoning of profits into luxury consumption, financial assets and obscure financial products. This regulation is necessary for the promotion of investment in socially useful infrastructure and in green technologies that contribute to employment creation and well-being for the many, and not just for the few. To assist this process, national banks capable of carrying out long-term investments could be established if governments were reluctant to invest directly themselves.

The GND makes full employment a direct target of economic policy because, together with long-term investment, this will have the greatest impact on gender equality, well-being and positive macro-economic outcomes. Employment is important since it provides a means of inclusivity and, if it is regular, reliable and properly paid, it will help to reduce inequality and gender inequality. When jobs are scarce, discrimination against women increases; but decent wages will help to increase labour's share of value added, which has been falling consistently over the last four decades. This emphasis on public investment and employment creation is critically important if the massive amounts of public money that are being spent on trying to prevent economic collapse after COVID-19 are to contribute towards building more inclusive and sustainable economies and societies.

The GND does not challenge capitalism but attempts to unlock the 'creative impulses of markets' while 'controlling their more destructive tendencies', though it is arguable whether this degree of control would be politically acceptable to those currently in power. Yet without such control it is doubtful whether the GND would be capable of meeting the SDGs or the sustainable and equitable outcomes it seeks to achieve.[27] Nonetheless, if some of its recommendations and changes are implemented, the world would be profoundly different.

While the GND provides an overarching framework, Plan F and the purple economy develop in greater detail the thinking about gender equality and the environment.

Feminist Plan F

Plan F was developed by the Women's Budget Groups (WBGs) in England and Scotland and relates specifically to these two economies, English and Scottish; but the underlying ideas have wider applicability. Plan F 'is a long-term vision for a prosperous and caring economy focused on investment in social infrastructure such as health, education, childcare, social housing and lifelong care, which benefit all, not just the few'.[28]

Like the GND, Plan F rejects austerity and supports recovery through state-led stimulus programmes and through increased public investment and public spending in the real economy. It differs from the GND in that it is grounded in feminist economics, and therefore more critical of market societies and of the atomistic key protagonist thought to generate creative and optimal outcomes. It recognises instead the interdependent character of human decision-making and the need for societies to make conscious policy choices. Just like the GND, Plan F predated the COVID-19 crisis, yet there are regular updates to it and its recommendations remain relevant, as it seeks to establish a care-led green recovery.[29]

The key elements of Plan F are

1 to increase public spending on social protection and public services, especially childcare, adult and social care, and support for survivors of domestic violence;
2 to improve working conditions and pay; strengthen workers' rights and bargaining

powers; redress growing labour precarity and in-work poverty by ensuring living wages; and ensure that parental leave programmes enable women and men to engage in caring and community activities;

3 to increase public investment in social and physical infrastructure – including the caring industries, health and education, green technologies and social housing.

Few of these elements were evident in the United Kingdom's post-coronavirus recovery strategy, even though unprecedented amounts of money were pumped into the economy. The recovery programme built upon the UK 2020 Budget,[30] which proposed a major physical infrastructure programme, predominantly roads, rail and telecoms, though some money was allocated for building schools and hospitals. The new proposal[31] added considerable support for job creation and training, especially for young people, and some of this was targeted towards green issues and social care. But the scale of this funding was substantially lower than the physical infrastructure programme announced in the Budget. While funds were given to boost the property sector and to support the leisure and hospitality sectors via temporary reductions in VAT and subsidies for dining out, nothing was done to assist the growing numbers of people living in poverty and dependent on food banks. Other countries, for instance France and Germany, used the stimulus to finance a green new deal, and Denmark offered no support to companies that used tax havens; but little attention has been given to investing in social infrastructure anywhere.

Investing in social infrastructure contributes to gender equality by recognising, reducing and redistributing unpaid work and thus lifting the constraints on women's participation in the labour market.[32] It helps to create a healthier, better-educated and well-nurtured population and creates more employment than a comparable amount of investment in physical infrastructure. Until the last decade, the argument for investing in social infrastructure was largely theoretical, but an emerging body of analysis shows that such investment makes economic and social sense and contributes to greater gender equality. This evidence comes from various regions around the world, including South Africa, the Republic of Korea and Turkey.[33]

I focus here on the comparative impact analysis of investing in physical and in social infrastructure carried out by UK's WBGs.[34] The purpose of their study was to demonstrate the benefits of investing in social infrastructure: these are less widely known than the benefits of investing in physical infra-structure, an investment that often forms part of stimulus strategies.

The WBGs' study was carried out for the International Trades Union Congress and explores the employment impact of investing 2 per cent of GDP in the construction and caring industries for seven OECD countries: Denmark, Germany, Italy, the United Kingdom, Australia, Japan and the United States. A technique known as input–output analysis was used to identify the multiplier effect of the investment on the economy as a whole by cal-culating the number of jobs created in the caring or construction sectors themselves (i.e. the direct jobs), the jobs created in the sectors that supply goods and services to these sectors, such as beds or toys in care or bricks in construction (i.e. the indirect jobs), and the jobs created as a consequence of the newly employed workers spending their wages (i.e. the indirect effects).

If the investment took place in caring, then the majority of jobs created would be taken up by women; but, owing to expansion in other sectors, jobs in stereotypically male sectors would be cre-ated too. More specifically, while both forms of investment would generate increases in employ-

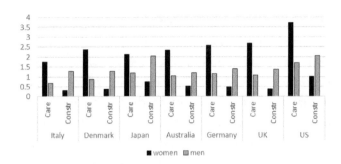

Figure 4.1. Comparative employment effects of investing in social and physical infrastructure

Source: Adapted from De Henau et al. (2016)
Note: The employment changes displayed reflect the consequence of investing 2 per cent of GDP in construction and care. Overall employment increases and increases among women are greater if the investment is in care.

ment, investment in care would create substantially more jobs overall, and up to four times as many jobs for women in Germany, Australia, the United Kingdom and the United States (see Figure 4.1). What is particularly interesting is that the overall number of jobs generated for men would be almost the same as it would be if the investment took place in construction; but, if the investment took place in construction instead of care, both the overall number of jobs and the number of jobs taken up by women would be substantially lower.

The analysis is based on the current gender division of labour between construction and care but, ideally, if the predicted expansion of these sectors occurred and appropriate training was provided, then their pay, conditions and gendering might become more equal. One criticism of this study is that the results are due to the lower pay in the care sector, but more recent analysis shows that, even if the pay levels were the same, more jobs would still be created if the investment took place in care.[35] An additional benefit of investing in care is that its initial effect is likely to be more carbon-neutral than the initial effect of investing in physical infrastructure.

A similar study of six 'emerging' economies – Brazil, China, Costa Rica, India, Indonesia and South Africa – also found that public investment in care-related sectors led to more employment overall than a parallel investment in physical infrastructure and that a higher proportion went to women, potentially narrowing the gender employment gap.[36]

Apart from creating new jobs and aiding economy recovery, investment in childcare and social care would help to resolve some of the central economic and social problems that confront contemporary societies: the deficit in care, demographic aging and the continuing gender inequality. Over time, the investment should also pay for itself, as a consequence of increased tax revenues from the newly employed people – and also by saving the cost of social protection, which would otherwise be required.

Despite this evidence and some recognition from international institutions such as UNCTAD, the significance of social infrastructure is not acknowledged in national accounting rules, which continue to favour investment in physical entities. Spending on physical infrastructure, which includes the wages of the building workers, is regarded as capital expenditure and considered acceptable because it generates returns in the long run. By contrast, while investment in the building of hospitals, schools and nurseries can count as capital investment and therefore be viewed as acceptable, the running of hospitals, schools and nurseries – and so the wages of the caring workers – counts as current expenditure, and therefore is restricted. Indeed, as discussed in chapter 2, it is primarily these areas that are cut by austerity policies. The thinking behind these categorisations is gender-biased, as it fails to recognise that investment in social infrastructure produces, among other things, long-term gains in the form of a population that is better educated, healthier and more cared for.

A partial exception comes from the Republic of Korea in the first years of the twenty-first century, when the government increased its support for child and adult social care in order to redress low economic growth and high unemployment, together with the social problems of low fertility and gender employment inequality. By combining this economic argument, which has instrumental force, with the non-instrumental case for investing in people, in other words with an argument that has intrinsic value in the sphere of social justice, the policy became acceptable in the eyes of very diverse political interests. However, in order to meet the IMF's loan conditions, the government committed to increasing labour market flexibility. In consequence the precise impact of the Korean measures on gender equality remains unclear: working conditions deteriorated, women continue to be overrepresented in the least secure jobs, and the gender pay gap remains.[37] So, while investing in social infrastructure is in principle capable of addressing economic problems and gender equality simultaneously, whether it does so in practice is highly contingent on the context in which it is introduced.

Plan F is also supportive of investment in physical infrastructure, especially in green technologies, but this aspect is given greater emphasis in the purple economy, which could bridge the divide between those who press for overcoming social injustice and those who stay focused on saving the environment.

The purple economy

There are two different versions of the purple economy: one, developed in France, emphasises the significance of the cultural economy; the other, developed by Ipek Ilkaracan, seeks to resolve the economic crisis, the ecological crisis and the crisis of care and to end austerity. The model is given the name of a colour to mirror the idea of a 'green' economy: just as green symbolises nature, purple resonates with the feminist movement.[38] Just like the feminist Plan F, the purple economy advocates a society that should have the following features:

1 a universal infrastructure of social care;
2 regulated labour markets designed to support the work–life balance, women and men having equal incentives to take leave and be involved in caring;
3 regulations of the macroeconomic environment for nature and nurture as key objectives;
4 an ecologically sound infrastructure, both

physical and social, that should include the needs of rural communities.[39]

Again like Plan F, the purple economy recognises the significance of social reproduction: this process represents one of the 'conditions of possibility' for economic and social life.[40] Thus, in an equitable and inclusive society, social infrastructure should be properly funded and supported by the state rather than depend on profit-seeking suppliers, who in turn rely on low-paid or unpaid female, minority and migrant labour; otherwise the inequalities related to gender, class and country of origin would be sustained.

In line with the advocates of a green economy, the proponents of a purple economy argue that the costs of caring should be paid for by 'internalising the externalities'. By this they mean that all the costs and benefits of these activities – including those that flow to people not directly involved in producing or consuming the specific products – would be taken into account and paid for.

In both care and the environment, there are costs and benefits that everyone experiences but not everyone pays for. Everyone suffers from pollution and climate change, but the people primarily responsible for creating the pollution or for contributing to climate change do not pay for these adverse effects. By the same token, if there are environmentally minded producers who implement green practices, many people will benefit; even those who do not consume a specific product will gain in a general way, so they, too, should contribute to that product. For example, conserving the Amazon rainforest would help the whole world, so the whole world should pay for this necessary process and ensure that the people living there enjoy a well-being of their own choice and of a standard comparable to that of people living elsewhere. By the same logic, everyone benefits from being surrounded by educated and well-cared-for people – hence everyone, not just parents, should contribute to the costs in some way.

Both Plan F and the purple economy predate COVID-19, but the fact that they contain key elements for supporting recovery from this crisis still makes them relevant after COVID-19. Governments around the world are spending billions of public money to restimulate economies, so there is a real opportunity to 'build back better' and in more inclusive ways. Central to this task is the provision of employment for the many people who will be made redundant from jobs that are no longer viable; so it is critical to invest in labour-intensive activities that can be created quickly, and here investment in social infrastructure and in green technologies could enable the economy to recover quickly and in more equitable and sustainable ways.

Financing alternatives

All the alternatives described here propose expanding public investment and expenditure; these would in part pay for themselves, through increases in employment and output that would create more tax revenue and would lower the costs of social protection. In addition, a series of progressive and gender-transformative tax policies could be introduced. Taxes on incomes could be more progressive; taxes on property, wealth, inheritance and financial transactions could be introduced or raised; tax havens could be eliminated and measures be taken to ensure that the existing taxes are collected effectively. Even very modest measures such as raising the tax rate by 5 per cent among the top 10 per cent of the population in the wealthiest 25 per cent of countries would raise almost as much as was spent on the Marshall Plan for the reconstruction of Europe in the mid-twentieth century.[41] And this measure would not even redress the decline in the tax rates on top incomes in the last four decades: in the United States, for example, they have fallen by 40 per cent since 1980.

These realistic, *ex post* redistributive taxes could be accompanied by measures designed to change the existing wage and salary structures, which are highly gendered and racialised and therefore lead to large gender and ethnic pay gaps. Not only were low-paid public sector workers adversely affected by austerity; many were suddenly transformed into key workers who played vital roles, risking their lives to sustain others through the coronavirus crisis. The momentum of public appreciation needs to be matched by a transformation of the wage structure as countries plan for a post-coronavirus future.

Conclusion

Austerity has gendered outcomes that are uneven and disadvantage women – BAME women in particular. In spite of this, until the COVID-19 pandemic, it continued to be introduced whenever and wherever countries fell into debt – even in the face of evidence that austerity policies rarely resolve the economic problems they purport to address.

In 2020 austerity was abandoned and displaced

by the largest public spending spree in history. Yet there is a real risk that, once the COVID-19 risk has faded, austerity would return with a vengeance, justifying drastic cuts by appeal to the need to pay for the public spending that had been aimed at tackling the virus. As Arundhati Roy argued, 'the world is facing a rupture . . . a portal, a gateway between one world and the next'.[42] Public spending could be used to build towards a sustainable and equitable future through investments in the real economy, in social infrastructure and in green technologies. Alternatively, it could be used to repair the old economy and to return to an inequitable 'business as usual'.

At present there is a momentum for change, a readiness to invest in public services and in the people who work in them, a desire to ensure that these key workers are rewarded in ways that reflect their importance to sustaining life, a sense of need to address gendered and racial inequalities, and a will to take measures so that global pandemics do not return, environmental disasters do not follow, and the world is made safer place for everyone.

There is no shortage of ideas about how to build a better future, so it is crucial that progressive academics find ways of brainstorming with activists to make the arguments for alternative policies better known to politicians, international institutions and populations at large. That way it will be possible to build consensus, or at least a majority support, for some of the very credible alternatives to austerity and more inclusive and sustainable models of development. In these discussions it is also critical that the ideas of feminist economists are not marginalised or forgotten. Only then will the future world be one in which the enduring problem of gender inequality is resolved.

Notes

Notes to Chapter 1

1 The terms 'corona' and 'COVID-19', which desig-
nate the disease produced by coronavirus, are used
interchangeably throughout this book.
2 Roy (2020: 214).
3 The UK Chancellor of the Exchequer Alistair Darling,
as quoted in Ireland (2011).
4 G20 is an international forum consisting of
Argentina, Australia, Brazil, Canada, China, the
European Union, France, Germany, India, Indonesia,
Italy, Japan, Mexico, Russia, Saudi Arabia, South
Africa, South Korea, Spain, Turkey, the United
Kingdom, and the United States.
5 Blanchard (2008).
6 Wintour and Rankin (2020).
7 Ortiz et al. (2015).
8 Ortiz et al. (2015).
9 Figures are calculated on the basis of Ortiz et al.
(2015).

10 See European Commission (2008), (2012).

11 Smith and Foley (2017).

12 Lagarde (2018).

13 IMF (2010: 4) see also Ortiz et al. (2015).

14 Krugman (2015).

15 Reinhart and Rogoff (2010).

16 Alesina and Ardagna (2010).

17 According to David Cameron, then leader of the Conservative Party in opposition; see Cameron (2009).

18 Ortiz et al. (2015).

19 See BBC 2 (2012): Paul Krugman patiently explains this difference to a disbelieving city financier and Conservative Party politician.

20 Musindarwezo and Jones (2019).

21 *Washington Post* (2016).

22 David and Rossi (2019).

23 IMF (2019).

24 Ortiz and Stubbs (2019).

25 UNCTAD [UN Conference on Trade and Development] (2017: 3).

26 IMF (2020b).

27 OECD (2020a). The OECD has forecast that the richer nations are likely to incur $17 trillion of public debt, the average debt-to-GDP ratio rising to 137 per cent of GDP.

28 *Financial Times* (2020b). In the United Kingdom, for example, between March and May 2020 the deficit has grown twice as large as after the 2007 financial crisis and the overall level of public debt has reached a higher level than in 1963, when the country was

still in the process of paying off debt accrued during the Second World War.

29 See Build Back Better (2020).
30 IMF (2020a).
31 Rainer (2020).
32 Al Jazeera News Video (2020).
33 Elson and Çağatay (2000).
34 In this book I treat gender in a binary way and make little reference to sexuality, since comparative evidence is limited at present, but see Lehtonen (2018) for a discussion with respect to the United Kingdom.
35 For a parallel remark, see Bair (2010: 204).

Notes to Chapter 2

1 Alston (2018).
2 Fawcett Society (2012).
3 Elson (2012).
4 UN Women (2019).
5 Kushi and McManus (2018).
6 UN Women (2019).
7 Akwugo and Bassel (2017).
8 Kabeer (2017).
9 UN Women (2020a).
10 Bhowmick (2020).
11 Kushi and McManus (2018).
12 International Labour Organization [ILO] (2020).
13 Bailey and West (2020).
14 UN Women (2019).
15 Kushi and McManus (2018).
16 King Dejardin (2009: 3).

17 UN Women (2019).
18 Furloughing is a process in which governments pay a proportion of workers' wages in order to encourage firms to retain their employees when workplaces closed. The United States and Japan provided some income to families, and India, Pakistan and the Republic of Korea have provided relief for the poorest.
19 IFS (2020).
20 IFS (2020).
21 Garikipati and Kambhampati (2020).
22 Braddick (2020).
23 WHO [World Health Organisation] (2020).
24 Nelson (2018).
25 ILO (2015); Ortiz et al. (2015).
26 Kushi and McManus (2018).
27 ONS [Office for National Statistics] (2019).
28 Laird (2017).
29 EPSU (2017).
30 Akintola et al. (2016).
31 TUC (2016).
32 Keates (2019).
33 McDonald and Baker (2020).
34 NHS (2020).
35 Baumol (1967).
36 In Japan robots are used in around 80 per cent of care homes and are reported to be quite popular among residents, as complements to rather than substitutes for human care (*Economist* 2017).
37 Baumol (1967).
38 National Audit Office (2018b).
39 LiGU (2014).

40 Boffey (2014).
41 Williams (2013).
42 In 2020, the discharge of elderly people from hospitals to care homes without testing for COVID-19 is widely thought to be responsible for the large number of COVID-19-related deaths in this sector.
43 EHRC (2011: 27–8).
44 Catton et al. (2019).
45 UN Women (2015: 20).
46 Elaine Yates from Coventry Haven giving evidence to the relevant all-party parliamentary group; see APPG (2015).
47 UN Women (2020c).
48 UN Women (2020b).
49 David (2018).
50 UK Parliament (2020).
51 Austin and Smith (2019).
52 Rhys et al. (2019).
53 Santos and Vieira (2018).
54 Gross (2018).
55 Work and Pensions Committee (2018).
56 Reed and Portes (2018).
57 CPAG (2018).
58 House of Commons Library (2017).
59 WBG [Women's Budget Group] et al. (2017).
60 De Henau and Reed (2016).
61 Alston (2018).
62 Trussell Trust (2018).
63 Cameron (2011).
64 Jensen and Tyler (2015).
65 Stuckler et al. (2017).

66 CESCR (1990: paragraph 10); see also Elson (2012).
67 Elson (2012).
68 Dunford (2015).
69 Elson (2012).
70 Alston (2019).
71 Booth (2019).
72 WBG (2018b).
73 WBG (2018c).
74 ONS (2020); Platt and Warwick (2020).
75 *Financial Times* (2020a).
76 Reuters (2020).
77 IMF (2020b).
78 UNCTAD (2017).

Notes to Chapter 3

1 Smith (1976: 10).
2 Hayek (1945).
3 Jevons (1911); Hayek (1945).
4 Smith (1976: 10).
5 Keynes (1924: 80).
6 Marçal (2016).
7 Hobbes (1998: 102).
8 Himmelweit (2007).
9 Rai et al. (2014).
10 IMF (2015).
11 Perrons and Plomien (2013).
12 Elson and Çağatay (2000: 1361–2).
13 Bhattacharya (2020).
14 Polanyi (1957).
15 Warren (2011).

16 Polanyi (1957).
17 Heller (2005).
18 IMF (2020a).
19 Hermann (2010).
20 Ortiz et al. (2015).
21 Bautzer (2020).
22 Hermann (2010).
23 Mathiesen (2015).
24 Rhys et al. (2019).
25 Originally proposed by James Tobin in 1972 for currency transactions, but now applied more broadly to financial transactions. To date, this tax has been implemented only in France, Belgium, Greece and Italy.
26 Ortiz et al. (2015).
27 WBG (2018a).
28 Ortiz et al. (2015).
29 Elson and Çağatay (2000).
30 Elson and Çağatay (2000).
31 Elson and Çağatay (2000: 1348).
32 Alston (2018).
33 Conley (2012).
34 Women and Equalities Select Parliamentary Committee (2016).
35 WBG (2018b).
36 Budlender, Sharpe and Allen (1998: 6).
37 Government of Canada (2018).
38 WBG (2020a).
39 European Parliament (2019).
40 Bettio et al. (2012).
41 This description is a gendered adjustment to the

UNDP [UN Development Programme] (2007) definition and my modification to a version created by Katy Ida – a student in the feminist economics class at the LSE in 2014.

42 John Loxley, quoted in Elson (2006: 120).

43 Sen (1998).

44 Krugman (2015).

Notes to Chapter 4

1 Guterres (2020).

2 Dearden (2017).

3 Carr (2020).

4 IMF (2020a).

5 Polanyi (2001: 149).

6 Hobsbawm (2008), quoted in Perrons and Plomien (2013: 6).

7 Taylor (2020).

8 See e.g. Bargawi et al. (2017); Karamessini and Rubery (2014); Blyth (2013).

9 Blanchard and Leigh (2013).

10 Stuckler and Basu (2013).

11 Heath and Cohen (2018).

12 Paraphrase of Joseph Stiglitz, quoted by the BBC; see BBC News (2020).

13 Alcoba and McGowan (2020).

14 Focus E15 Campaign (2020).

15 Open Democracy (2018).

16 IMF (2020c).

17 Musindarwezo and Jones (2019).

18 IMF (2020c); Eurodad (2020).

19 Salgado and Fischer (2020).
20 Musindarwezo (2019).
21 Musindarwezo and Jones (2019).
22 UNCTAD (2017).
23 UNCTAD (2017).
24 UNCTAD (2017: 163).
25 UNCTAD (2017: 152 and ii – in this order).
26 In this respect the GND draws explicitly on the work of the WBG for ITUC (De Henau et al. 2016).
27 UNCTAD (2017: 147).
28 Pearson and Elson (2015: 26).
29 WBG (2020b). WBG (2020c) provides a post-COVID plan for a caring economy.
30 UK Gov. (2020a).
31 UK Gov. (2020b).
32 Elson (2017).
33 Antonopoulos and Kim (2011) for South Africa and the Republic of Korea; Ilkkaracan et al. (2015) for Turkey.
34 See De Henau et al. (2016) for selected OECD countries and De Henau et al. (2017) for emerging economies.
35 De Henau and Himmelweit (2020).
36 De Henau et al. (2017).
37 Peng (2011).
38 Ilkkaracan (2016).
39 Ilkkaracan (2016: 8).
40 Fraser (2014: 550).
41 UNCTAD (2017).
42 Roy (2020).

Bibliography

Akintola, O., Gwelo, N., Labonté, R. and Appadu, T. (2016) The global financial crisis: Experiences of and implications for community-based organizations providing health and social services in South Africa. *Critical Public Health* 26(3): 307–21.

Akwugo, E. and Bassel, L. (2017) Whose crisis counts? Minority women, austerity and activism in France and Britain. In J. Kantola and E. Lombardo, eds, *Gender and the Economic Crisis in Europe: Politics, Institutions and Intersectionality*. London: Palgrave Macmillan, pp. 185–208.

Al Jazeera News Video (2020) Coronavirus: Worldwide applause for front-line medical staff. https://www.aljazeera.com/programmes/newsfeed/2020/03/coronavirus-worldwide-applause-frontline-medical-staff-200330111116862.html.

Alcoba, N. and McGowan, C. (2020) NiUnaMenos five years on: Latin America as deadly as ever for women, say activists. *Guardian*, 4 June. https://www. theguardian.com/global-development/2020/jun/04/ niunamenos-five-years-on-latin-america-as-deadly- as-ever-for-women-say-activists.

Alesina, A. and Ardagna, S. (2010) Large changes in fiscal policy: Taxes versus spending. *Tax Policy and the Economy* 24: 35–68.

Alston, P. (2018) UN special rapporteur on extreme poverty and human rights: Preliminary findings, visit to the United Kingdom. Press Conference, London 16 November. https://www.youtube.com/watch?v= 5XeV_CTIh3c.

Alston, P. (2019) UN special rapporteur on extreme poverty and human rights: Final report, visit to the United Kingdom. http://www.bristol.ac.uk/poverty-institute/ news/2019/un-rapporteur-final-report.html.

Antonopoulos, R. and Kim, K. (2011) Public job-creation programs: The economic benefits of investing in social care? Case studies in South Africa and the United States. Working Paper No. 671, Levy Economics Institute.

APPG (2015) *The Changing Landscape of Domestic and Sexual Violence Services*. All-Party Parliamentary Group on Domestic and Sexual Violence Inquiry. https://1q7dqy2unor827bqjls0c4rn-wpengine.netdna- ssl.com/wp-content/uploads/2015/11/APPG_Report_ 20151.pdf.

Austin, R. and Smith, K. (2019) Nowhere to turn.

Bibliography

Women's Aid. https://www.womensaid.org.uk/res earch-and-publications/nowomanturnedaway.

Bailey, S. and West, M. (2020) Ethnic minority deaths and COVID-19: What are we to do? King's Fund. https://www.kingsfund.org.uk/blog/2020/04/ethnic-minority-deaths-covid-19.

Bair, J. (2010) On difference and capital: Gender and the globalization of production. *Signs: Journal of Women in Culture and Society* 36(1): 203–26.

Bargawi, H., Cozzi, G. and Himmelweit, S., eds (2017) *Economics and Austerity in Europe: Gendered Impacts and Sustainable Alternatives*. London: Routledge.

Baumol, W. (1967) Macroeconomics of unbalanced growth: The anatomy of urban crisis. *American Economic Review* 57(3): 415–26.

Bautzer, T. (2020) Brazil government aims to sell at least $20 billion in assets this year. Reuters, 29 January. https://www.reuters.com/article/us-brazil-privatiza-tion/brazil-govt-aims-to-sell-at-least-20-billion-in-assets-this-year-idUSKCN1PN1O4.

BBC 2 (2012) Is austerity always the best policy? Newsnight, 31 May. https://www.bbc.co.uk/news/av/business-18281669/is-austerity-always-the-best-policy.

BBC News (2020) You can't ask people to die: Coronavirus woes deepen Argentina's crisis. 31 May. https://www.bbc.co.uk/news/world-latin-america-52846939.

Bettio, F., Corsi, M., Ippoliti, C. d', Lyberaki, A., Samek Lodovici, M. and Verashchagina, A. (2012)

Bibliography

The impact of the economic crisis on the situation of women and men and on gender equality policies. European Commission Synthesis Report.

Bhattacharya, T. (2020) Social reproduction and the pandemic. *Dissent*, 2 April. https://www.dissentmagaz ine.org/online_articles/social-reproduction-and-the-pandemic-with-tithi-bhattacharya.

Bhowmick, N. (2020) 'They treat us like stray dogs': Migrant workers flee India's cities. *National Geographic*, 27 May. https://www.nationalgeog raphic.com/history/2020/05/they-treat-us-like-stray-dogs-migrant-workers-flee-india-cities.

Blanchard, O. (2008) IMF spells out need for global fiscal stimulus (Interview). *IMF Survey Magazine*, 29 December. https://www.imf.org/external/pubs/ft/sur vey/so/2008/INT122908A.htm?mod=article_inline.

Blanchard, O. and Leigh, D. (2013) Growth forecast errors and fiscal multipliers. IMF Working Paper 13/1. https://www.imf.org/external/pubs/ft/wp/2013/wp1301.pdf.

Blyth, M. (2013) *Austerity: The History of a Dangerous Idea*. Oxford: Oxford University Press.

Boffey, D. (2014) The care workers left behind as private equity targets the NHS. *Observer*, 9 August. https://www.theguardian.com/society/2014/aug/09/care-wor kers-private-equity-targets-the-nhs.

Booth, R. (2019) UN poverty expert hits back over UK ministers' 'denial of facts'. *Guardian*, 24 May. https://www.theguardian.com/society/2019/may/24/

un-poverty-expert-hits-back-over-uk-ministers-denial-of-facts-philip-alston.

Braddick, I. (2020) Angela Merkel praised for 'superb' explanation on how coronavirus infection rates impact healthcare systems. *Evening Standard*, 16 April. https://www.standard.co.uk/news/health/angela-merk el-infection-rates-explanation-a4416231.html.

Bretton Woods Project (2020) The IMF and World Bank-led Covid-19 recovery: 'Building back better' or locking in broken policies? Bretton Woods Observer, Summer 2020. https://www.brettonwo odsproject.org/wp-content/uploads/2020/07/BWP ObserverSummer2020.pdf.

Build Back Better (2020) The campaign for a coronavirus recovery plan that builds back better. https://www. buildbackbetteruk.org.

Budlender, D., Sharpe, R. and Allen, K. (1998) How to do a gender-sensitive budget analysis: Contemporary research and practice. https://www.femtech.at/sites/ default/files/How_to_do_a_gender-sensitive_budget_a nalysis.pdf.

Cameron, D. (2009) Labour has maxed out our credit card. https://www.conservativehome.com/thetorydia ry/2008/11/labour-has-maxe.html.

Cameron, D. (2011) Speech on Welfare Reform Bill. 17 February. http://www.number10.gov.uk/news/spe eches-and-transcripts/2011/02/pms-speech-on-welfare reform-bill-60717.

Bibliography

Carr, P. (2020) Returning to 'normal' post-coronavirus would be inhumane. The Conversation, 13 May. https://theconversation.com/returning-to-normal-post-coronavirus-would-be-inhumane-136558.

Catton, S., Conti, G., Farquarson, C. and Ginja, R. (2019) The health effects of sure start. Institute of Fiscal Studies. https://www.ifs.org.uk/uploads/R155-The-health-effects-of-Sure-Start.pdf.

CEDAW [Convention on the Elimination of All Forms of Discrimination against Women] (2017) General recommendation No. 35 on gender-based violence against women, updating general recommendation No. 19. https://tbinternet.ohchr.org/Treaties/CEDAW/Shared%20Documents/1_Global/CEDAW_C_GC_35_8267_E.pdf.

CESCR [Committee on Economic, Social and Cultural Rights] (1990) General Comment No. 3: The nature of states parties' obligations. https://www.ohchr.org/EN/ProfessionalInterest/Pages/CESCR.aspx.

CESR [Centre for Economic and Social Rights] (2018) Austerity in the midst of inequality threatens human rights: Fact sheet 18. http://www.cesr.org/sites/default/files/FACTSHEET-Artwork-Online-Nov%206%20FINAL.pdf.

Conley, J. (2012) Using equality to challenge austerity: New actors, old problems. *Work, Employment and Society* 26(2): 349–59.

CPAG [Child Poverty Action Group] (2018) Something

needs saying about universal credit and women: It is discrimination by design. https://cpag.org.uk/news-blogs/news-listings/something-needs-saying-about-universal-credit-and-women-%E2%80%93-it-discrimination.

David, G. (2018) The impacts of IMF-backed austerity on women's rights in Brazil. Bretton Woods Project. https://www.brettonwoodsproject.org/2018/03/impacts-imf-backed-austerity-womens-rights-brazil.

David, G. and Rossi, P. (2019) Why Brazil's permanent austerity policy is harming its economic future. openDemocracy. https://www.opendemocracy.net/en/oureconomy/why-brazils-permanent-austerity-policy-harming-its-economic-future.

De Henau, J. and Himmelweit, S. (2020) Stimulating OECD economies post-Covid by investing in care. Open University Working Paper 85. http://www.open.ac.uk/ikd/sites/www.open.ac.uk.ikd/files/files/working-papers/COVID%20care-led%20recovery_IKD_WP85_2020_06_12%20%28003%29.pdf.

De Henau, J. Himmelweit, S. and Perrons, D. (2017) *Investing in the Care Economy: Simulating Employment Effects by Gender in Countries in Emerging Economies.* ITUC. https://www.ituc-csi.org/investing-in-the-care-economy.

De Henau, J. Himmelweit, S., Łapniewska, Z. and Perrons, D. (2016) *Investing in the Care Economy: A Gender Analysis of Employment Stimulus in Seven*

OECD Countries. ITUC. https://www.ituc-csi.org/
IMG/pdf/care_economy_en.pdf.

De Henau, J. and Reed, H. (2016) A cumulative gender
impact assessment of ten years of austerity policies.
WBG Briefing Paper. http://wbg.org.uk/wp-content/
uploads/2016/03/De_HenauReed_WBG_GIAtaxben_
briefing_2016_03_06.pdf.

Dearden, L. (2017) Theresa May prompts anger after tell-
ing nurse who hasn't had pay rise for eight years: 'There's
no magic money tree.' *Independent*, 3 June. https://
www.independent.co.uk/news/uk/politics/theresa-may-
nurse-magic-money-tree-bbcqt-question-time-pay-rise-
eight-years-election-latest-a7770576.html.

Donald, K. and Lusiani, N. (2017) The gendered costs of
austerity: Assessing the IMF's role in budget cuts which
threaten women's rights. Bretton Woods Project. https://
socialprotection-humanrights.org/wp-content/uploa
ds/2017/10/Gendered-Costs-of-Austerity-2017.pdf.

Dunford, R. (2015) Peasant activism and the rise of food
sovereignty: Decolonising and democratising norm dif-
fusion? *European Journal of International Relations*
23(1): 145–61.

Economist (2017) Japan is embracing nursing-care
robots. 23 November. https://www.economist.com/
business/2017/11/23/japan-is-embracing-nursing-ca
re-robots.

EHRC (2011) *Close to Home: An Inquiry into Older
People and Human Rights in Home Care*. Equality

and Human Rights Commission. https://www.equalit yhumanrights.com/sites/default/files/close_to_home. pdf.

Elson, D. (2006) *Budgeting for Human Rights*. New York: UNIFEM.

Elson, D. (2012) The reduction of the UK budget deficit: A human rights perspective. *International Review of Applied Economics* 26(2): 177–90.

Elson, D. (2017) Recognise, reduce and redistribute unpaid carework. *New Labour Forum* 26(2): 52–61.

Elson, D. and Çağatay, N. (2000) The social content of macroeconomic policies. *World Development* 28(7): 1347–64.

EPSU [European Public Service Union] (2017) Pay in the public services: How workers continue to pay for the crisis. https://www.epsu.org/sites/default/files/article/files/EPSU-ETUCE%20Briefing%20Pay%20in%20the%20Public%20Services%20-%20EN.pdf.

Eurodad (2020) Six things you should know about Covid-19 and debt for developing countries. https://eurodad.org/covid19-debt-FAQ.

European Commission (2008) A European economic recovery plan. https://ec.europa.eu/economy_finance/publications/pages/publication13504_en.pdf.

European Commission (2012) Tackling the financial crisis. http://ec.europa.eu/competition/recovery/financial_sector.html.

Bibliography

European Commission (2018) Stability and Growth Pact.
https://ec.europa.eu/info/business-economy-euro/eco
nomic-and-fiscal-policy-coordination/eu-economic-
governance-monitoring-prevention-correction/stabili
ty-and-growth-pact_en.

European Commission (2019) European Pillar of Social
Rights: Building a more inclusive and fairer European
Union. https://ec.europa.eu/commission/priorities/dee
per-and-fairer-economic-and-monetary-union/europ
ean-pillar-social-rights_en.

European Parliament (2019) Gender mainstreaming in
the EU: State of play. http://www.europarl.europa.
eu/RegData/etudes/ATAG/2019/630359/EPRS_ATA
(2019)630359_EN.pdf.

Eurostat (2015) File: Public balance and general government debt, 2011–14 (% of GDP) YB15 II.png.
Eurostat: Statistics Explained. http://ec.europa.eu/eur
ostat/statistics-explained/index.php/File:Public_bal
ance_and_general_government_debt,_2011%E2%80
%9314_(%C2%B9)_(%25_of_GDP)_YB15_II.png.

Fawcett Society (2012) The impact of austerity on
women. 19 March. https://www.fawcettsociety.org.
uk/the-impact-of-austerity-on-women.

Financial Times (2020a) India's biggest slum tests Modi's
coronavirus response. 24 April. https://www.ft.com/
content/5199e04b-d235-49e2-a20c-af7bb8fc53a9
(available on subscription).

Financial Times (2020b) Treasury paper sets out stark

Bibliography

UK options to cut estimated £337bn deficit. 12 May. https://www.ft.com/content/f0c7ab6d-33ba-4777-8d d8-0960a78a556a (available on subscription).

Focus E15 Campaign (2020) Why are 3 empty tower blocks next door to an overcrowded hostel in Newham? https://focuse15.org/2020/06/29/why-are-3-empty-tower-blocks-next-door-to-an-overcrowded-hostel-in-newham.

Fraser, N. (2014) Can society be commodities all the way down? *Economy and Society* 43(4): 541–58.

Garikipati, S. and Kambhampati, U. (2020) Leading the fight against the pandemic: Does gender 'really' matter? *Centre for Economic Performance* 26: 1–16.

Government of Canada (2018) Equality and growth. https://www.budget.gc.ca/2018/home-accueil-en.html.

Gross, A. (2018) Brazil austerity policies devastating to rural communities: Analysis, Mongabay. https://news.mongabay.com/2018/08/brazil-austerity-policies-deva stating-to-rural-communities-analysis.

Guterres, A. (2020) The recovery from the COVID-19 crisis must lead to a different economy. https://www.un.org/en/un-coronavirus-communications-team/la unch-report-socio-economic-impacts-covid-19.

Hayek, F. (1945) The uses of knowledge in society. *American Economic Review* 45(4): 519–30.

Heath, M. and Cohen, L. (2018) Argentina unveils 'emergency' austerity measures, grain export taxes. Reuters News. https://www.reuters.com/article/us-argentina-economy/argentina-unveils-emergency-aust erity-measures-grain-export-taxes-to-balance-budget-idUSKCN1LJ156.

Heller, P. (2005) Back to basics: Fiscal space: What it is and how to get it. *Finance and Development: A Quarterly Magazine of the IMF* 42(2). http://www. imf.org/external/pubs/ft/fandd/2005/06/basics.htm.

Hermann, C. (2010) The marketization of health care in Europe. *Socialist Register* 46: 125–44.

Himmelweit, S. (2007) The prospects for caring: Economic theory and policy analysis. *Cambridge Journal of Economics* 31(4): 581–99.

Hobbes, T. (1998) [1641] *On the Citizen*, translated and edited by R. Turk and M. Silvert Horne. Cambridge: Cambridge University Press.

House of Commons Library (2017) Estimating the gender impact of tax and benefits changes. Briefing papers SN06758. https://researchbriefings.parliament. uk/ResearchBriefing/Summary/SN06758.

IFS (2020) How are mothers and fathers balancing work and family under lockdown? Institute of Fiscal Studies. https://www.ifs.org.uk/publications/14860.

Ilkkaracan, I. (2016) The purple economy complementing the green: Towards sustainable and caring economies. Paper presented at the Levy Economics Institute and Hewlett Foundation Workshop. http://www.levy institute.org/news/gender-andmacroeconomics-work shop-2016.

Bibliography

Ilkkaracan, I., Kijong, K. and Kaya, T. (2015) The impact of public investment in social care services on employment, gender equality and poverty: The Turkish case. Levy Bard Institute. http://www.levyinstitute.org/pubs/rpr_8_15.pdf.

ILO (2015) *World Employment and Social Outlook: The Changing Nature of Jobs*. https://www.ilo.org/global/research/global-reports/weso/2015-changing-nature-of-jobs/WCMS_368626/lang--en/index.htm.

ILO (2020) ILO Monitor: COVID-19 and the world of work: Second edition. https://www.ilo.org/wcmsp5/groups/public/---dgreports/---dcomm/documents/briefingnote/wcms_740877.pdf.

IMF (2010) *Strategies for Fiscal Consolidation in the Post-Crisis World*. https://www.imf.org/external/np/pp/eng/2010/020410a.pdf.

IMF (2015) *Causes and Consequences of Income Inequality: A Global Perspective*. IMF staff discussion note written by Era Dabla-Norris, Kalpana Kochhar, Nujin Suphaphiphat, Frantisek Ricka and Evridiki Tsount. https://www.imf.org/external/pubs/ft/sdn/2015/sdn1513.pdf.

IMF (2018) *Global Financial Stability Report*. https://www.imf.org/en/publications/gfsr/issues/2018/09/25/global-financial-stability-report-october-2018.

IMF (2019) Debt distress factsheet. https://www.imf.org/external/Pubs/ft/dsa/DSAlist.pdf.

IMF (2020a) IMF executive board approves a US$739

million disbursement to Kenya to address the impact of the COVID-19 Pandemic. Press release. https://www.imf.org/en/News/Articles/2020/05/06/pr20208-kenya-imf-executive-board-approves-us-million-disbursement-address-impact-covid-19-pandemic.

IMF (2020b) IMF policy tracker: Policy responses to COVID-19. https://www.imf.org/en/Topics/imf-and-covid19/Policy-Responses-to-COVID-19.

IMF (2020c) Transcript of the April 2020 Fiscal Monitor press briefing. https://www.imf.org/en/News/Articles/2020/04/15/tr041520-transcript-of-the-april-2020-fiscal-monitor-press-briefing.

Ireland, S. (2011) Alistair Darling: We were two hours away from the cash points running dry. *Independent*, 18 March. https://www.independent.co.uk/news/people/profiles/alistair-darling-we-were-two-hours-from-the-cashpoints-running-dry-2245350.html.

Jensen, T. and Tyler, I. (2015) 'Benefits broods': The cultural and political crafting of anti-welfare common sense. *Critical Social Policy* 35(4): 470–91.

Jevons, W. (1911) [1871] *The Theory of Political Economy* (4th edn). London: Macmillan.

Kabeer, N. (2017) Economic pathways to women's empowerment and active citizenship: What does the evidence from Bangladesh tell us? *Journal of Development Studies,* 53(5): 649–63.

Karamessini, M. and Rubery, J., eds (2014) *Women and Austerity: The Economic Crisis*

Bibliography

and the Future for Gender Equality. Abingdon: Routledge.

Keates, C. (2019) Teachers spending their own money to buy pupils food and clothes. *Metro*, 19 April. https://metro.co.uk/2019/04/19/teachers-spending-money-buy-pupils-food-clothes-9264654.

Keynes, J. M. (1924) *A Tract on the Monetary Reform.* London: Macmillan.

Keynes, J. M. (1973) The marginal propensity to consume and the multiplier. In J. M. Keynes, *The General Theory of Employment, Interest and Money.* Basingstoke: Macmillan and St Martin's Press for the Royal Economic Society, pp. 113–31 (= Book 3, chapter 10).

Keynes, J. M. (1982) *Collected Writings*, vol. 21: *Activities, 1931–39; World Crises and Policies in Britain and America*, edited by D. Moggridge. Cambridge: Macmillan and Cambridge University Press.

King Dejardin, A. (2009) Gender (in)equality, globalization and governance. ILO Working Paper 92. https://www.ilo.org/wcmsp5/groups/public/---dgreports/---integration/documents/publication/wcms_108648.pdf.

Klein, N. (2019) *On Fire: The Burning Case for a Green New Deal.* London: Allen Lane.

Krugman, P. (2015) The austerity delusion: The case for cuts was a lie: Why does Britain still believe it?

Guardian, 29 April. http://www.theguardian.com/busi
ness/ng-interactive/2015/apr/29/the-austerity-delusion.

Kushi, S. and McManus I. (2018) Gendered costs of austerity: The effects of welfare regime and government
policies on employment across the OECD, 2000–13.
International Labour Review 157(4): 557–87.

Lagarde, C. (2018) Ten years after Lehman: Lessons
learned and challenges ahead. IMF blog. https://blogs.
imf.org/2018/09/05/ten-years-after-lehman-lessons-
learned-and-challenges-ahead.

Laird, J. (2017) Public sector employment inequality in the United States and the Great Recession.
Demography 54: 391–411.

Lehtonen, A. (2018) *The Sexual and Intimate Life of UK
Austerity Politics*. PhD thesis, LSE. http://etheses.lse.
ac.uk/3800.

LiGU (2014) *Key to Care: Report of the Burstow
Commission on the Future of the Home Care
Workforce*. https://openaccess.city.ac.uk/id/eprint/136
13/1/KeyToCare%5B1%5D.pdf.

Marçal, K. (2016) *Who Cooked Adam Smith's Dinner?
A Story about Women and Economics*. London:
Portobello Books.

Mathiesen, K. (2015) Germany's hypocrisy over Greece
water privatisation. *Guardian*, 14 August. https://
www.theguardian.com/sustainable-business/2015/
aug/14/germanys-hypocrisy-over-greece-water-privati
sation.

McDonald, M. and Baker, C. (2020) Nursing workforce shortage in England. House of Commons Library. https://commonslibrary.parliament.uk/research-briefings/cdp-2020-0037.

Musindarwezo, D. (2019) Realising women's rights: The role of public debt. Gender and Development Network, Briefings, August. https://gadnetwork.org/gadn-news/2018/8/9/new-briefing-realising-womens-rights-the-role-of-public-debt-in-africa?rq=public%20debt.

Musindarwezo, D. and Jones, T. (2019) Debt and gender equality: How debt-servicing conditions harm women in Africa. https://www.brettonwoodsproject.org/2019/04/debt-and-gender-equality-how-debt-servicing-conditions-harm-women-in-africa.

National Audit Office (2018a) The adult social care workforce in England. https://www.nao.org.uk/press-release/the-adult-social-care-workforce-in-england/#.

National Audit Office (2018b) Financial sustainability of local authorities 2018. https://www.nao.org.uk/wp-content/uploads/2018/03/Financial-sustainabilty-of-local-authorites-2018.pdf.

Nelson J. (2018) *Gender and Risk Taking: Economics, Evidence and Why the Answers Matter*. London: Routledge.

Nelson, J. (2019) *Economics for Humans* (2nd edn). Chicago, IL: University of Chicago Press.

NHS (2020) Thousands of former NHS staff are back

on the front line in the NHS fight against coronavirus. https://www.england.nhs.uk/2020/04/thousands-of-former-nhs-staff-are-back-on-the-front-line-in-the-nhs-fight-against-coronavirus.

OECD (2016) Employment: Female share of public and total employment. OECD Employment Data. http://stats.oecd.org/index.aspx?queryid=54754.

OECD (2020a) OECD updates G20 summit on outlook for global economy. http://www.oecd.org/newsroom/oecd-updates-g20-summit-on-outlook-for-global-economy.htm.

OECD (2020b) Tax and fiscal policy should continue to support households and businesses through containment, then shift to bolstering recovery. https://www.oecd.org/tax/tax-and-fiscal-policy-should-continue-to-support-households-and-businesses-through-containment-then-shift-to-bolstering-recovery.htm.

ONS (2019) Public sector employment, UK: June 2019. https://www.ons.gov.uk/employmentandlabourmarket/peopleinwork/publicsectorpersonnel/bulletins/publicsectoremployment/june2019.

ONS (2020) Deaths involving COVID-19 by local area and deprivation. https://www.ons.gov.uk/peoplepopulationandcommunity/birthsdeathsandmarriages/deaths/datasets/deathsinvolvingcovid19bylocalareaanddeprivation.

Open Democracy (2018) 10 years of women's resistance to austerity across Europe, in pictures. https://www.

opendemocracy.net/en/5050/10-years-of-womens-resistance-to-austerity-across-europe-in-pictures.

Ortiz, I. Cummings, M., Capaldo, J. and Karunanethy, K. (2015) The decade of adjustment: A review of austerity trends 2010–2020 in 187 countries. ESS Working Paper No. 53. http://www.social-protection.org/gimi/gess/RessourcePDF.action?ressource.ressourceId=531 92.

Ortiz, I. and Stubbs, T. (2019) More austerity for developing countries: It's bad news, and it's avoidable. Consortium News, 3 December. https://consortiumn ews.com/2019/12/03/more-austerity-for-developing-countries-its-bad-news-and-its-avoidable.

Pearson, R. and Elson, D. (2015) Transcending the impact of the financial crisis in the United Kingdom: Towards plan F: A feminist economic strategy. *Feminist Review* 109: 8–30.

Peng, I. (2011) The good, the bad and the confusing: The political economy of social care expansion in South Korea. *Development and Change* 42(4): 905–23.

Perrons, D. (2015) Gendering the inequality debate. *Gender and Development* 23(2): 207–22.

Perrons, D. and Plomien, A. (2013) Gender, inequality and the crisis: Towards more sustainable development. In M. Karamessini and J. Rubery, eds, *Women and Austerity: The Economic Crisis and the Future for Gender Equality*. Routledge: Abingdon, pp. 295–313.

Bibliography

Piketty, T. (2014) *Capital in the Twenty-First Century*. Cambridge, MA: Harvard University Press.

Platt, L. and Warwick, R. (2020) Are some ethnic groups more vulnerable to COVID-19 than others? IFI Briefing Note. https://www.ifs.org.uk/publications/14827.

Polanyi, K. (1957) *Trade and Market in the Early Empires; Economies in History and Theory*. Glencoe, IL: Free Press.

Polanyi, K. (2001) [1944] *The Great Transformation: The Political and Economic Origins of our Time*. Boston, MA: Beacon Press.

Rai, S., Hoskyns, C. and Thomas, D. (2014) Depletion. *International Feminist Journal of Politics* 16(1): 86–105.

Rainer, G. (2020) Exclusive: Treasury blueprint to raise taxes and freeze wages to pay for the £300bn Coronavirus bill. *Daily Telegraph*, 12 May. https://www.telegraph.co.uk/politics/2020/05/12/exclusive-treasury-blueprint-raise-taxes-freeze-wages-pay-300bn.

Reed, H. and Portes, J. (2018) *The Cumulative Impact on Living Standards of Public Spending Changes*. EHRC Report 120. https://www.equalityhumanrights.com/sites/default/files/cumulative-impact-on-living-standards-of-public-spending-changes.pdf.

Reinhart, C. and Rogoff, K. (2010) Growth in a time of debt. *American Economic Review* 100: 573–8.

Reuters (2020) Factbox: Global economic policy

response to coronavirus crisis. https://www.reuters.com/article/us-health-coronavirus-economy-factbox/factbox-global-economic-policy-response-to-coronavirus-crisis-idUSKCN21W2AJ.

Rhys, O., Barnaby, A., Roe, S. and Wlasny, M. (2019) *The Economic and Social Costs of Domestic Abuse.* Home Office Research Report 107. https://assets.publishing.service.gov.uk/government/uploads/system/uploads/attachment_data/file/772180/horr107.pdf.

Robinson, J. (1955) Marx, Marshall and Keynes. In J. Robinson, *Contributions to Modern Economics.* Oxford: Basil Blackwell, pp. 61–75.

Roy, A. (2020) *Azadi: Freedom, Fascism, Fiction.* London: Penguin

Salgado, A. and Fischer, A. (2020) Ecuador, COVID-19 and the IMF: How austerity exacerbated the crisis. Bliss. https://issblog.nl/2020/04/09/covid-19-ecuador-covid-19-and-the-imf-how-austerity-exacerbated-the-crisis-by-ana-lucia-badillo-salgado-and-andrew-m-fischer.

Santos, I. and Vieira, F. (2018) The right to healthcare and fiscal austerity: The Brazilian case from an international perspective. *Ciência & saúde coletiva* 23(7). http://www.scielo.br/scielo.php?pid=S1413-812320 18000702303&script=sci_arttext&tlng=en.

Sen, A. (1998) Human development and financial conservatism. *World Development* 26(4): 742–73.

Skidelsky, R. (2012) Printing money and tax cuts aren't enough: We need real investment. *New Statesman,*

1 March. http://www.newstatesman.com/economy/20 12/03/investment-government-policy.

Smith, A. (1976) [1776] *The Wealth of Nations*. Chicago, IL: University of Chicago Press.

Smith, S. and Foley, S. (2017) Bailout costs will be a burden for years. *Financial Times*, 8 August. https://www.ft.com/content/b823371a-76e6-11e7-90c0-90a 9d1bc9691.

Stuckler, D. and Basu, S. (2013) *The Body Economic: Why Austerity Kills*. New York: Basic Books.

Stuckler, D., Reeves, A., Loopstra, R., Karanikolos, M. and McKee, M. (2017) Austerity and health: The impact in the UK and Europe. *European Journal of Public Health* 27(4): 18–21.

Taylor, M. (2020) How change happens. BBC Radio 4, 24 June. https://www.bbc.co.uk/programmes/m000 kdv2.

Trussell Trust (2018) Is universal credit truly universal? https://s3-eu-west-1.amazonaws.com/trusselltrust-doc uments/Trussell-Trust-Left-Behind-2018.pdf.

TUC [Trades Union Congress] (2016) Lift the cap: A fair deal for public sector workers. https://www.tuc. org.uk/research-analysis/reports/national/lift-cap-fair-deal-public-service-workers.

UK Gov. (2020a) Budget 2020: Documents. https://www.gov.uk/government/publications/budget-2020-docum ents.

UK Gov. (2020b) A plan for jobs, 2020. https://www.

gov.uk/government/topical-events/a-plan-for-jobs-2020.

UK Parliament (2020) Home Office preparedness for COVID-19 (coronavirus): Domestic abuse and risks of harm within the home. https://publications.parliam ent.uk/pa/cm5801/cmselect/cmhaff/321/32102.htm.

UN (2019) Sustainable Development Goals. https://www.un.org/sustainabledevelopment/sustainable-dev elopment-goals.

UN Human Rights (2018) Effects of foreign debt and other related financial obligations of States on the full enjoyment of all human rights, particularly economic, social and cultural rights. https://documents-dds-ny. un.org/doc/UNDOC/GEN/G17/364/96/PDF/G1736 496.pdf?OpenElement.

UN Women (2015) Progress of the world's women, 2015–2016: Transforming economies, realizing rights. https://www.unwomen.org/en/digital-library/publicat ions/2015/4/progress-of-the-worlds-women-2015.

UN Women (2019) Facts and figures: Economic empow-erment. http://www.unwomen.org/en/what-we-do/eco nomic-empowerment/facts-and-figures.

UN Women (2020a) Addressing the impacts of the COVID-19 pandemic on women migrant workers. https://www.unwomen.org/-/media/headquarters/ attachments/sections/library/publications/2020/guid ance-note-impacts-of-the-covid-19-pandemic-on-wom en-migrant-workers-en.pdf?la=en&vs=227.

Bibliography

UN Women (2020b) COVID-19 and ending violence against women and girls. https://www.unwomen.org/-/media/headquarters/attachments/sections/library/publications/2020/issue-brief-covid-19-and-ending-violence-against-women-and-girls-en.pdf?la=en&vs=5006.

UN Women (2020c) Impact of COVID-19 on violence against women and girls and service provision: UN Women rapid assessment and findings https://www.unwomen.org/-/media/headquarters/attachments/sections/library/publications/2020/impact-of-covid-19-on-violence-against-women-and-girls-and-service-provision-en.pdf?la=en&vs=0.

UNCTAD (2017) *Trade and Development Report 2017: Beyond Austerity: Towards a Global New Deal.* http://unctad.org/en/pages/PublicationWebflyer.aspx?publicationid=1852.

UNDP (2007) Primer: Fiscal space for MDGs. https://sarpn.org/documents/d0002584/Fiscal_Space_UNDP_Jun2007.pdf.

Warren, E. (2011) There is nobody in this country who got rich on his own. CBS News. https://www.cbsnews.com/news/elizabeth-warren-there-is-nobody-in-this-country-who-got-rich-on-his-own.

Washington Post (2016) Brazil passes the mother of all austerity plans. 16 December. https://www.washingtonpost.com/news/worldviews/wp/2016/12/16/brazil-passes-the-mother-of-all-austerity-plans.

Bibliography

WBG (2018a) Analyses of UK budgets. https://wbg.org.uk/analysis/assessments.

WBG (2018b) The impact of austerity on women in the UK. Submission to the UNHRC. https://wbg.org.uk/wp-content/uploads/2018/02/UN-contribution-The-Impact-of-Austerity-on-Women-in-the-UK-Feb-2018.pdf.

WBG (2018c) Universal credit risks increasing women's vulnerability to abuse. https://wbg.org.uk/media/universal-credit-risks-increasing-womens-vulnerability-to-abuse-say-womens-groups.

WBG (2020a) Crises collide: Women and COVID-19. Examining gender and other equality issues during the coronavirus outbreak https://wbg.org.uk/wp-content/uploads/2020/04/FINAL.pdf.

WBG (2020b) WBG response to chancellor's 'economic update'. https://wbg.org.uk/media/wbg-response-to-chancellors-economic-update.

WBG (2020c) Creating a caring economy: A call to action: Report of the Commission on a Gender-Equal Economy. https://wbg.org.uk/wp-content/uploads/2020/09/CGEE-Creating-a-Caring-Economy-A-Call-to-Action-WBG.pdf.

WBG and Runnymede Trust, with Reclaim and Coventry Women's Voices (2017) *Intersecting Inequalities: The Impact of Austerity on Black and Asian Women in the UK.* https://www.runnymedetrust.org/uploads/Press Releases/Correct%20WBG%20report%20for%20Microsite.pdf.

Bibliography

Williams, Z. (2013) No offence: This is – no offence –
the worst idea a person in government has ever had.
Guardian, 2 February. https://www.theguardian.com/
money/2013/feb/01/liz-truss-tried-six-toddlers.

Wintour, P. and Rankin, J. (2020) G20 leaders issue
pledge to do 'whatever it takes' on coronavirus.
Guardian, 26 March. https://www.theguardian.com/
world/2020/mar/26/g20-leaders-issue-pledge-to-do-
whatever-it-takes-on-coronavirus.

Women and Equalities Select Parliamentary Committee
(2016) Equalities analysis and the 2015 Spending
Review and Autumn Statement https://publications.
parliament.uk/pa/cm201617/cmselect/cmwomeq/825/
82504.htm#_idTextAnchor006.

Women's Aid (2019) Nowhere to turn: Findings from
the third year of the No Woman Turned Away project.
https://1q7dqy2unor827bqjls0c4rn-wpengine.netdna-
ssl.com/wp-content/uploads/2019/09/Nowhere-to-
Turn-2019-Full-Report.pdf.

Work and Pensions Committee (2018) PIP and ESA
Inquiry.   https://publications.parliament.uk/pa/cm20
1719/cmselect/cmworpen/355/35504.htm#footnote-
007.

WHO (2020) Coronavirus Disease Dashboard. https://
covid19.who.int/?gclid=Cj0KCQjw4f35BRDBAR
IsAPePBHynYtvxmPGeMF8M-VqjR0jRdfRkauJ
dPOxCE8HER3QHHFXyHavWs84aAhR3EALw_
wcB.